WOMEN'S SEXUAL FANTASIES

INTRODUCTION

I wrote *Female Sexual Fantasies* (aka *Freely Female*) in London in 1971, shortly after the advent of the famed contraceptive pill which liberated women sexually, and before the outbreak of AIDS which put an end to the make love, not war season.

It was a historic book as it was the first one in our time to broach the subject.

I have to confess that it all started because I wanted to earn some money as a writer, and asked myself, what sells? Sex, of course sells, but what hadn't been done as yet? Ah, women's sexual fantasies hadn't been explored. I certainly knew a lot about those, seeing as I practically never had sex without thinking up elaborate 'dirty' scenarios while I was doing it.

With such a 'hot' idea I soon found a publisher who gave me a decent advance, and so, armed with tape recorder, curiosity, enthusiasm, and considerable apprehension, I set out to interview many women from different walks of life, and stepped into a labyrinth of euphemisms, revelation, truth, laughter, sorrow and words. Along with the masses of words I detected an undercurrent of warning – words are distortions, contradictions, hazards. The sentences we've been taught automatically shape our notions and label our emotions. And most often the idioms we've been unconsciously indoctrinated with formulate the patterns of our life-style. I tried to avoid these traps and pitfalls as I endeavoured to arrive at each meeting fresh, without preconceived notions, and let the individual talk freely, and in so doing reveal both herself and her sexual fantasies.

I took it for granted I would have no trouble gathering a bouquet of carnal *Scheherazade* stories, and hey presto, the erotic best-seller would be on bookshelves. I was wrong. As I found myself unwittingly stepping into lives that I had not given much thought to, I very soon discovered that most of the women I met lived their mundane existence without fantasy, and this reflected in their sexuality.

It's rare to hear tales of perfumed gardens by chemically sedated housewives, bored-to-death, establishment teachers or robotized secretaries. Most often I encountered simply the real need to talk, share secrets, ask questions.

I was at that period fully partaking in the Swinging London's *zeitgeist*, and such women as the dissatisfied spouse of a blue-collar worker, or an aging suburban housewife did not fit into my bohemian scene. *My* life abounded with fantasy and I never considered that there were lives void of it. And then my eyes opened.

I became a feminist then, when, due to the interviews, I become conscious of the hardships of both ordinary women and not-so-ordinary women. As my research proceeded my heart went out to the women whose secret confessions I heard. I wrote about each one with affection and gave more space to their life stories than I had originally planned, and more than the erotic book I'd originally envisioned, it turned out to be women talking about their sexuality.

It soon became clear to me that the nature of my own fantasy life was not unique, that multitudes of women shared the masochistic orientation: degradation, brutalization, flagellation, slave images which are so much a part of their role. I felt that if women could verbalize them and share them, perhaps it would serve to clarify both their own sexual identity and to what degree these fantasies are a product of male domination and, therefore, not genuinely their own.

In the end I wrote this book in an attempt to discover and relay female sexual needs. I wanted to penetrate the barriers erected by men who often, in their fear and ignorance of women, arrogantly define female function, and in so doing, dehumanize both women and themselves.

The women arrived organically – one sent the other. They all wanted to talk – for the majority this would be the first time they could speak openly about their sexual fantasies. I was privileged to be able to give them a voice.

There was shyness and self-doubt to be reckoned with, and the dominant presence of the silent machine recording allegedly uncensored tales. But I found most of the women to be open, empathetic, trusting. Sometimes the meeting were brief and superficial, others developed into lasting friendships. And this book is their end product.

I wrote, at the time, in heated anger at the structures of a system which uses sex to manipulate. Most people are duped about their own sexuality – misguided by ignorance, distortion and societal taboos. Sex is not the brutal, obscene beast parents, teachers, and the likes of establishment religionists would have us believe, but a magnificent, energetic life-force representing continuity through loving.

Loving is the most intense experience available to us: primal, basic, ecstatic, transcendent.

Sex is a vital components of the self and as its primary manifestation sexuality cannot be satisfied merely by fucking – the cunt/prick syndrome. When isolated from, rather than incorporated into the total human phenomenon, sexual intercourse leads to disintegration of the self; when allowed to flow freely it finds expression in all things.

Everything in nature celebrates sexuality. Penetration of sunbeams, reception of raindrops, fury of lightening, caress of smiles, stamens of flowers, paw of the tiger, speed of the stallion, shape of touch, lapping of waves, stars, moon, currents, love, cunt, cock, tits, skin, are all parts of an overriding energy system whose base is genital: reception/penetration, penetration/reception, the final communion, the maker of life.

I'm not a sexologist and this is not a thesis on the whys and wherefores of sexual fantasy. But I have some personal thoughts on it. I tend to believe that if the fantasy occurs because the woman is emotionally compelled to have it, if it's a stand-in for the sexuality she feels from within, or if she uses the image because there are some aspects of her psyche which cannot be realized, it could be a problem. On the other hand, if a woman has never experienced an orgasm, I feel she should conjure up images that excite her. Because to know what the orgasm experience is like, even if induced by fantasy, might be what the woman needs to guide herself into it instinctively, without thought.

But we are all fundamentally different and for each one of us our sexuality is personal and unique. What goes for one does not necessarily go for another, so in the end, it's up to the individual to understand what her particular need and proclivity is.

As I said, these interviews were conducted in the early seventies; much has changed since then. Certainly the vernacular has. I toyed with the idea of editing the woman's stories, bringing some aspects more up to date, but finally decided to leave them as they are. This way the book also retains the flavour of the times and in some ways becomes a reference thesis.

When I decided to republish my book, naming it this time *Women's Sexual Fantasies*, it was suggested to bring it up to date and interview some modern women. I pondered about it, but finally determined against it, as I'm sure I would have concluded that the more it changes the more it stays the same; and in the end I don't think I would have stumbled across anything all that different or new. A lot of women still want to be dominated, others are into dominatrix; some still have fantasies about their sons or their fathers, others want to find themselves with a truck driver on a lonely country road, and many still have fantasies about making it with their own sex, even though we are now in an era where this is permitted, albeit still looked upon critically in certain milieus and in organized religion.

Maybe the only modern fantasy would have to do with sex over the internet. The one person I talked to about it, said that she was totally disillusioned with the whole procedure. I'm sure there are others enjoying cyber romances that induce them to have erotic thoughts (and talks) with whoever is on the other line. But, in the end, although the scenarios might differ the fantasies remain fundamentally the same.

I have, nevertheless, made some changes. For one, when the book was published by ACE Books in 1972, many of the conversations were edited by the publisher, the women's stories cut, and only their fantasies were printed. Also some of the women were omitted altogether. I have now printed my original interviews and added the one's who were left out.

I have also added three new interviews which I recorded in later years, after the book was published. I think they are interesting.

One with Judith Malina, (the co-founder with Julian Beck of the renowned Living Theatre) who I interviewed in Rome in the Spring of 1979 (part of this interview was published in *Harpers and Queen* in London in July 1979, as well as in *Resurgence*, in December 1979.

In the early eighties I interviewed Molly Parkin, after meeting her in the Chelsea Art's Club.

The third with the psychiatrist, R.D. Laing. Laing I interviewed in London in 1984. (The piece was published in 1997 by Bob Mullan in a collection of stories about Laing: *R. D. Laing: Creative Destroyer.*)

I believe this is a book of learning value to both women and men. Women will identify with some of the characters and perhaps learn from others. Men who take it seriously and look into it further than just for erotic satisfaction will get an insight into women's sexuality.

THE WOMEN

Alice

Barbara

Caroline

Cynthia

Dianah

Donna

Elizabeth

Fiore

Gillian

Gwen

Ingrid

Iris

Judith Malina

Laura

Louise

Marie-Anne

Mary

Molly Parkin

Mona

Monica

Roina

Sagittarian

Sally

Teresa

Valery

Veronica

Virginia

Yvonne

R.D. Laing

ALICE

I met Alice at the historic Glastonbury Music Festival in 1971. She'd been living in a rural commune, and after both the relationship with her lover and the commune dispersed, she set out on the road with her four month old baby, a tent and a carpet bag.

She lives without money, relying on the generosity of others. It's easy to give to her – some milk, fruit, a loaf of bread . . .

She is looking for the answers which will make the dream come true. Trying to find clues in spirituality, looking towards India – a thirteen-year-old guru to give her knowledge.

Gentle, strong, clear eyes, wide smile, burnished dark hair, with radiant love for the gurgling little girl who bounces on her healthy, sun-tanned shoulders; she dances barefoot on soft grass, arms outstretched towards the orange-lollipop sun – towards the ducks that glided in formation in the cloudless sky. Her milk filled breasts overflow her peasant blouse.

She said one thing no other woman I'd spoken to had said: "I think that fallen breasts are very beautiful, because it means you've had a child. You've given life. The more children you have the more they drop the more beautiful they look."

****

"We'd been stationary for the winter in a commune in Wales, and all the winter he spent repressing me and talking to me as if I was just a little girl, not treating me as a woman even though I'd just had his child, you know. And I found I was projecting images on him, things I wanted him to be but, you know, he would not be. And it seemed like I became my mother and he became his father, and the fights and arguments we had just became a classic – two people in a council house with their new child. The squabbles that *we* had, *every* couple had. I know because I asked and it's a repeat story. And he got violent and I got mentally violent and we reached the stage when our essences repelled and so we had to split and go away for some years, maybe to grow and develop ourselves and meet again – on the other side of time.

"With men there's this big thing about women often becoming their mothers and there's this feeling that their mothers are emasculating them, feeding off their energy. Mothers do that to their sons, if they haven't fulfilled it with their husbands – if it hasn't been a good thing . . . if it's been frustrated. And the whole cycle is being repeated generation after generation because the frustrated love that she has for her man goes into her son and she sacrifices her son's future.

"He's got a lot of hang-ups. He doesn't feel very confident and often we'd make love and he couldn't come. So he began lavishing affection on every chick that came in and I used to be so incredibly jealous, so jealous that I would hit my head against a brick wall. And he knew that I wanted to express how much I loved him by making love to him, but he would always make excuses and not let me, and spent days making music with other people, and then he'd come to bed and make love for a few minutes and then just roll over and go to sleep.

"And I was so hurt because I always felt that he was a very incredible person. His whole potential was so incredible but he was so fucked up and I knew that he'd been doing that to me because he'd been doing it to his mother; and all he wanted was love and attention and understanding. And it was ridiculous because I knew he felt a need but couldn't express it. And he had so much frustrated love in him that he had to express it, and so he expressed it with everyone else, which was beautiful, but you know, in the end I felt that that's the way it should be – that it should go to other people now.

"Yet he wouldn't believe *I* didn't want to make love with anyone else – I think he wanted me to deep down inside him – but he wouldn't accept it because he was also so desperately jealous. Like I couldn't go in the street with him because all the time he would turn, looking, watching to see if I was looking at another man, and if a man came into the house he'd say, you want to fuck him, why are you looking at him like that, why do you sexually assess all the men you see? And he'd just be talking about himself, all the things he felt about women, because we always do that – project ourselves onto someone else until we learn not to do that.

"I think all the struggle in the world since it began has been through two opposites which you see in men and women – the struggle between the positive and the negative. And the same struggle happens with one person – the two opposite elements in their heads – the man and the woman. And not until you fuse these opposites and free yourself of the conflict that you are having with yourself, will you be able to make love . . . with yourself. It's yourself that you're seeing in the other person. But it's not really *your* essence you're seeing – it's your mother and your father left in you . . .

"You know how at first meetings, when a man and a woman click together, so called love at first sight – when you recognize your anima in the other person and you see each other, and it's really beautiful. But then ego gets in the way and you find you can't make love so beautifully anymore. And this all connects with the female and male sexual organs, because each person has got both – one less developed than the other. But if you're having a conflict inside you, and usually what happens inside your head manifests itself on a physical level, it's going to affect how you make love too.

"I believe that the whole thing is to fuse those opposites and I feel that in this age that's what we're going to do.

"Apparently all the children born after seventy-five are going to be born telepathic. In seventy-five all the planets are going to be in line – Juniper, the Earth, the Moon, Uranus who normally moves freely. All of them are dotted at different angles now, but they are all going to be in line and there's going to be a total eclipse and there's will be a powerful energy coming through and some are going to harness it . . . and there's going to be paradise on earth.

"I think in the years to come, in the next few years, people ought to prepare themselves physically and mentally to receive this energy. All the people who are sufficiently clear and sufficiently pure will be able to handle this energy and will be able to direct it into certain channels to enable the change to take place – the change in consciousness. "Everybody will be in the same mood at the same time. I think this festival is just an acid flash of what is going to happen for real. You know I was dancing and I wasn't following the music at all, it was as if the music was following me, my dance. I don't know how to describe it or evaluate it or even talk about it. It's like science fiction in a way. East is going to meet West, and we're going to get to another point. You know, like putting a triangle on the ground and if you pyramid it for the right and the left sides to meet . . . that's when you get into a new dimension of consciousness . . .

"I believe you maintain this consciousness through love, because when people make love in tune, when you bring Kundalini to the top of your head, your astral bodies get very close to each other and you can maintain the energy and vibration. I think it's much more significant making love with someone than we realize. My fantasy of love is that it's a communication on all levels, not only centred round the sexual organs. It's a very spiritual thing. It's two people completely in tune so that every single movement is felt and has a different meaning. I believe you can get divine awareness by making yourself completely in tune so that your bodies are united and you make yourself like a channel for awareness to come through you . . ."

BARBARA

The afternoon was amusing: I enjoyed her chat. But eventually the light, speedy monologue about herself, the lack of depth, and the often shallow superficiality began to weary me.

Her game is seduction. Sensuous, sensitive, very attractive, she looks boyish: tall, slender, small-bosomed, narrow-hipped, blonde haired. Undulating in her movement she projects a snake-like quality. Very pale, almost bloodless skin tightly drawn over high cheeks. Tenacious eyes look for mine. Her caressing touch is weightless and cold.

Despite the frequent peals of laughter I feel a great sadness about her.

****

"Well, the whole length of time I've been fucking, which is about nine or ten years now (I'm twenty-four now) three quarters of the time I've fucked . . . I've fucked for other people, not for me. You know . . . I wonder if this is normal? I've had this thing that if somebody has come on to me, I've felt, well, if I don't fuck them, well that's really being very ungenerous. Although I don't want to, I've done it; and I'll never, ever, ever, put a guy down when he's fucked me, like say . . . oh you know, you're no good. I couldn't do that. Yes, I have a great respect for men, I think. Even if they're really awful I don't think it's a bad thing; I'll always pretend, pretend that . . .

"I've got all the ingredients for a good whore, probably. I mean I just blend in everything, simply because I'm not looking for anything.

"It's a bad thing in me that I don't have any aims . . . goals. It's this very destructive thing. I don't know why I say this but I feel it's quite a destructive force not to have a goal, so therefore I just, like feed off everything else. I'm lazy, I also need financial support: which is a bit of a drag to me, really. I wish I didn't, because if I had money I'd enjoy myself more. I have to sort of give in a bit, with people, to get them to looking after me with money, whereas if I was independent . . .

"It's only very recently that I was able to like men that liked me. For a long, long time, as soon as somebody responded to me I'd say . . . sort of . . . go away. But then the last year I've started to become more interested in people, you know, people rather than fucking machines.

"But I think I'm a late developer as far as it goes in the head, because I'm so used to using my body, and getting anything I want with my body that I never thought, never ever consciously thought about anything till I went to Formentera and had the first relationship with a man. You know

I've lived with them before but I couldn't call it a relationship; but he was a really nice guy and because I was feeling better about myself I was able to have a really nice thing with him.

"Academically I'm stupid: that part of my brain doesn't register. I've lived off my wits, because I don't have anything concrete that I can fall back on . . . I write a lot of romantic drivel poetry. I would be ashamed to show it to anybody. I've always written poetry like that . . . I think I'd like to be famous . . .

"I'd like somebody to appreciate me, the alter me, I'd like to do something, yeah . . . I've dabbled in the theatre on and off all the time . . . I can assume any role, any role they like.

"I left school at fifteen. Even then I wasn't into it consciously; I was playing up to the boys. That was more important than exams, and I was the one who had to be funny and make the class laugh, so they all stop work. I was always being caned, terrible, all the teachers hated me.

"My father was a registered schizophrenic and he was mad all the time. He finally killed himself two years ago. He was . . . groovy . . . fuck . . . I never realized it until he died. He was brought up before the British Medical Council and shown as a case. All his life he always wanted to be a playboy. He didn't have any bread but he'd be out with the best, the richest. He was a really good con man. And any money he did get, he used to buy other people drinks and stuff like that. Of course my mother was very practical, very together. And she used to get us to side with her, right, which I realize now, was fucking terrible, but I didn't know it then.

"When he died it was like a major event in my life, almost a turning point. My father was very, very, very sexual and my mother was . . . she divorced him and he died a year later because he couldn't see the kids in the divorce. One of the reasons she put up for divorce was because he tried to commit buggery and he tried to make her take his thing in her mouth.

"When he died he was completely mad, completely. He just used to sit with a blanket around him, watching television. He wouldn't speak.

"I always imagine that he's going to come back. I'm really frightened of ghosts . . . I'm always aware of them: visiting, invisible, freaky and things. The night freaks me out, because I just know that I'm going to look around and there he's going to be there and I don't know how he's going to react to me. I really wish I'd been more sensitive than I was. I just didn't talk to him because my mother used to say, don't talk to your father because he doesn't give us any money, and that means we can't have any tea.

"She's alright, my mother's alright, but I wish she could see further than her nose, but she can't because she's been stifled for about twenty years. She's given up on me. I went home and I said, now listen – I had a heart to heart with her – I said, I want to talk to you. I said, look, I take drugs. I felt I had to do something to just make her jolt. I said, I've been taking a *lot* of drugs. She said, oh have you dear, well as long as you don't bring it home to me. I said, not only that, but I've been living off guys because I've no money. She said: you're just like your father. My mother never showed emotion

"I had a baby when I was seventeen . . . had it adopted, because of my parents. But looking back now, it was probably a good thing. I'm really pleased that I had a child, because if you have one, even if it's adopted, every woman should have a child, just for . . . the whole thing. Everybody should experience childbirth, one should – it's such an incredible physical experience. I don't even care so much about the child – it's selfish, I know. I'm very selfish. I care about the physical feeling I have, how clever I am; look what I've done. I'm probably very emotionally cold.

"I've never fucked anybody with a . . . what do you call it? I've only . . . sucked them and made them come. But when I've had chicks I'm always the male side of it . . . every chick I've ever made it with has had multiple orgasms. I always know how to use my fingers, because I know how to use fingers on myself so I think she's exactly the same as me so it's quite easy. It's very, very easy. Chicks are much easier than men; I like them a lot more. But I can never get romantically or passionately involved with a chick because they always turn round and start depending on me, you know.

"There was this chick in Formentera . . . she used to have a lot of orgasms, all night through. We made love whenever we could and she said, you're so much better than any man. And then she started to become . . . to look up to me. I hate that, I can't stand it. As soon as they start to respond it makes me become very cold.

"I've been fucking much longer with men than chicks. I've only been into chicks for a very short time. About a year. Physically into them, I mean. Never even thought about it before. Wasn't till I started taking lots of acid that I started really to dig chicks. I found that I was out looking for them. I don't know which I like best, I really don't know; I like them both. I always find that when I fuck with chicks I get to such a point . . . that then I'd like somebody to fuck me. You know, like ideally, one of each, if you can get it right.

"But it's so difficult to get into that sort of thing nicely without jealousies affecting you. I think I've been into about two scenes where it's been . . . just nice . . . nobody's been jealous of anybody else.

"I only had a scene with two guys once, and they were both . . . more homosexual. I mean they were bisexual but more inclined towards men. That was awful, and they were both fucking me, right, and I knew, I mean I could feel that one of those guys liked the guy more than me and one of them was doing the whole thing because it was the thing to do. I mean the whole thing wasn't spontaneous . . . it wasn't organic . . . it was organized.

"I'm one of those chicks who doesn't think about fucking. I don't see somebody and think ohhh, I can imagine him coming inside me and thrusting and throbbing. I never have that; it doesn't start until I actually touch the person . . . never in my head. People must have big pricks as well . . . but I don't like fucking for hours and hours. I used to when I was younger, now I find it too much. I mean I can have orgasms very easily.

"When I masturbate I have to keep my mind very concentrated, think about absolutely nothing. Like I can look at the wall, but as soon as I start thinking about anything, having a fantasy about anything, it's over. I'm completely unable to do anything; I won't come or anything.

"The only fantasy I've ever had . . . well there's two actually, but they're sort of . . . the first one is like . . . I design this bedroom in my mind. It's circular and it's made of panelled mirrors. In the beginning the panels slide aside and you come into a big circle of mirrors, and then you walk about three feet, you look down and there's another big circle of mirrors. At the bottom is a bed of feathers, and to get from the top, you have to jump into the feathers. It's very practical because all these mirrors slide back, and everything you need, like music and Kleenex (I'm very practical) is all behind these mirrors.

"I suppose it's a very housey thing, I don't want to be fucked in the middle of the desert. Although I'd quite like a pine forest, you know, because I like the smell of pine.

And the other one is . . . I've got a big thing about Bob Dylan.

"I think that I'm being so creative and different from everybody else . . . that there's a switch somewhere on me and I can make myself exactly whatever personality I want to be. So if I'm fantasizing about Bob Dylan, I can make myself into exactly what he's always wanted, all of his life, so like . . . he'd be complete: mind and body. As soon as he saw me, he'd recognize in me everything he's wanted. He'd only like, switch me, and I'd be exactly what he wanted. But during this fantasy I have, I know he's married, and I know he's got four kids, and in this fantasy I always work it out so his wife will fall in love with somebody, and she'll forget about him, so nobody gets hurt in the whole process.

"And then I build up my romantic thing of the way we meet and what we do. But I tend to fantasize about myself rather than about other people. I always want to be incredibly beautiful; I want to be the most beautiful thing that ever walked on the face of the earth.

"Do you know what my fantasy is really, really? I'd like to live somewhere, with a guy, and I'd like the guy to think exactly the same as I did, and I'd like to be surrounded by a lot of people and plenty of dope, and no problems about money.

"I'd really like to be with a guy and have some sort of solidarity there. Or would I . . .?"

CAROLINE

Twenty nine, pretty in a non-startling way, she's a clear-skinned, fair English rose. Elegantly tall her waist is trim, her ankles are thick and she chain smokes.

Caroline stems from the same background as Diana; many of their mannerisms and idioms are the same, but the two women don't have much in common. Dianah is an artist, she's imaginative and creative, and to a large extent has escaped her upbringing whilst rigid Caroline has remained attached to her upper-class culture and is trapped on a tree-lined street in a large Georgian house expensively decorated according to general ideas of feminine taste, by an interior designer.

We chat informally over a cup of tea amidst comfortable settees, generous couches, silks, brocades, pastel colours, vases filled with long-stemmed roses and distinguished works of art. Dainty side-boards house treasures: a bust in bronze of herself, impressive photographs of the royalty she's entertained and other precious family heirlooms.

Expressing herself in posh accent, her language is sexual and forth-coming: she easily talks about fucking and cunts, but I had the feeling that that which was deep in her was never made manifest. She seemed to be in total control, and only her birth mark, the port-wine stain on her neck, which reddened as our talk becomes more intimate, revealed her nervousness.

****

"I was born and brought up in the country . . . sort of upper-class educated at a private school; didn't go to the university and wished I had. Instead I did, you know, all those awful coffee bar jobs. And of course I was a deb., which was the most humiliating thing anyone could have gone through; because all those men were the sort of men who rode horses. They didn't want sex objects in their girls, they wanted success objects.

"They wanted their girls to be very pretty, very much written up in the newspapers, very rich. They wanted them to have fathers who gave big dances, but more than anything they didn't want them to have ideas or conversation. You had to have jokes and you had to have small talk, but you just couldn't have any ideas at all; and so you felt totally irrelevant and inadequate and useless; and it was the most humiliating thing. The anguish . . . it really was ghastly. They have been brought up to expect that the whole world revolves around them.

"Their mother revolves around them because they're probably going to inherit some big house, some estate or family firm, or go into the family regiment. They only have about four jobs:

which is running their family estates, being in the family regiment, being in industry – but not really, because that's not quite okay – and being in the city. So they're brought up to think the world revolves around them, including all the girls that they meet. And of course all the girls do revolve around them.

"I mean they're perfectly nice. Really, they're rather too rich. They've all been educated at Eton, which actually I think is very nice, though some other very nice people have been educated at public schools.

"It's a fact that in English shires where they hunt a lot, people change wives and husbands frequently, yearly, annually. They are the sort of people who are rich enough that they don't have to have jobs and they have time – it all goes together with that sort of life. It's perfectly easy to go off to the south of France for a couple of weeks with anyone who happens to be around.

"I think to have a very good sexual fantasy you have to have a marvellous imagination. Or a very bad sex life. And most women have very bad sex lives . . . until they're about twenty-seven. I didn't have an orgasm until I was about that age, and then my sex life became great fun.

"I used to masturbate before I had orgasms, but I think I had some sort of tiny orgasms when I masturbated. I remember when I read Fanny Hill – that was wildly exciting. But I think it was really very sort of minor masturbation.

"Sex for me is just straightforward; it's not something particularly exotic or strange or rare. It's not at all sort of special or different. I mean I feel quite friendly about fucking. There's people I like, probably one's known them, you're fond of them and you still find them quite attractive and so probably you go to bed and maybe then you won't see them again – that's rather my philosophy. But when I have something very good and big, then it's just that, and I tend to be quite faithful when there is somebody, a main person, then that's the only person; but when there isn't . . . I like to have fantasies, you know.

"I think that most people who like to be excited and frightened by riding horses also like sex and men and fucking. The thrill of going over big fence after big fence is absolutely blinding, you know; I mean it's a trip, you know. You don't think, like you don't think in bed.

"I have a very strong thing about horses. I had a fantastic father – and suspect I still have hang-ups about him. He was killed when I was six years old. He had race horses and was very attractive and very smashing and very artistic and quite sort of rare and extraordinary; and I have a very sort of ordinary and prosaic mother who brought us up on the legend of my father. One of the things that she thought we had to have in our lives because it was what my father would have wanted, was horses. From the very earliest age we were indoctrinated with this sort of creed of the horse.

"Now I know that the two things that turned me on are both very much to do with my father. One is a very good looking man with long legs, on a horse. But it's a sort of romantic fantasy as opposite to a sexual fantasy. I mean, my fantasy man is still a man who rides horses awfully beautifully: like Mr. Rochester in Jane Eyre. As you ride into the dusk with a frightfully good looking long-legged man on his horse, you are in a sort of different age. It's sort of nostalgic; it's very sort of Victorian or Edwardian. But it's a romantic fantasy.

"I mean it's not very exotic at all. When I see a beautiful man on a beautiful horse I think, what a sexy sight; I mean how terribly lovely, how marvellous he looks. But once he's off the horse he's usually no good because I know all he'll talk about is his boring horse and his sports car, so you know the fantasy ceases. There's not future to it because once he's off the horse it's lost its point. I mean the fact is you can't take the horse to bed with you.

"When one was a child one loved them like a doll. It was a terribly soppy relationship and one wanted to be protective and caring, until around puberty when the actual thing of the saddle in one's crutch happens. By the time I was about eleven one was conscious of the masturbatory function of the saddle: very hard, and it's absolutely in your cunt and you can't get away from it – if you ride well it's right there. I mean that's what you sit on, you sit absolutely astride on the saddle, you have your legs spread wide, so it becomes a very exciting sexual feeling. It was a very satisfactory feeling that one encouraged.

"The two total releases that I know are – one is sex straightforward and the other is riding a horse across country. You don't think, you absolutely feel. Your life can be in ruins and yet you go on and you're absolutely released. It's total naked emotion: you are frightened, you are exhilarated, you just *are*.

"You are controlling something which is wild and dangerous and difficult through one's skill in the saddle – it's a power that you are controlling through tact and skill – it's something that is a million times stronger and bigger and more dangerous than you. And the better and more gentle you're doing it the less strength it takes and the more successful you are in the domination of this creature. When you've got a stallion through a sound barrier, it floats, it feels like you've got something extraordinarily powerful on a piece of gossamer thread and there *you* are on top, controlling it. And you're riding down in the saddle, and there's pressure on your clitoris. And then the hurtling across the countryside, still terrifying yourself in this sort of sensual way. It's a sort of dance, a sort of jungle dancing you can control and you can do what you want with it – you know that it's all there under you, waiting to be realized. You hurtle off across a series of rather dangerous fences, hedges and walls, and I mean I'm quite frightened and it's like making love because like you don't think when you're experiencing an orgasm. And when you're riding for a long period, you're absolutely not thinking at all, you're simply experiencing and sensing . . . and then comes the orgasm.

"I wonder what it's like to actually sort of fuck a horse? I'm fascinated by it. I mean people don't actually fuck horses; or do they? A horse is so big . . . think of all those legs underneath and that fur in your mouth . . ."

CYNTHIA

Cynthia is a young housewife living in an impersonal, sparsely furnished one bedroom flat above a tobacconist's on the noisy High Street. Her husband Harry works at Tesco.

She wears a miniskirt that shows her pretty legs. Her body is agile, and there's a bright smile on her red-painted lips.

****

"My marriage was just a terrible mistake. I was very young and I just liked the idea of marriage; of having kids and looking after them. I don't know . . . I hate it. I mean what's housework, just picking up other people's shit?

"I was living at home and that wasn't any good, I didn't get along with my mum, and so I just sort of got married. It just sort of came naturally. We did get on very well, like brother and sister type of thing and it was really all right until I met Bob. I suppose we would have gone on for the rest of my life. But I suppose not . . . I suppose I was looking for someone else, I needed someone, in the position I was in.

"Harry hasn't got much life, and I wanted to be doing things all the time. He just sits here at night watching television – anything that's on, he'll just keep watching it, or just stare into space. I don't think he's ever read a book in his life. He's quite content to let things pass him by. He's in the same job for twelve years, since he's left school. To me he is dull and dreary and black and white, and that's what he is and I am not.

"And the thing is that my position isn't any different from the rest of the women on the High Street; it's just that I'm not going to wait around for years. I think everybody's been given a life, and that life is precious and you use it the best way you can, and to me it's just a waste, going on like this. It's a waste of life; it's a waste of two lives. Well, it's a waste of a lot of lives. There's Jenny – my friend – and Dave. She's married but she's having an affair with Dave. Ant there's Rose, who's around the corner, she's having an affair with Johnny, and there's Mary, over the road, she's having an affair with Albert. They're all at it, and it's all at the fire station.

"Firemen are notorious. Harry hates firemen, he really hates them. He hates it when they speak to me or wave across to me, because I know all of them, you know, and one of them might shout across to me good morning, and he says bloody firemen again.

"You see, there's a fire station at the back of the flats. Bob's a fireman there and I see him every day.

"There's three watches at the station: a red watch, a blue watch and a white watch. When one watch is off another is on. White watch play cards, red watch are drinkers – Bob's red watch – terrible drinkers, almost alcoholics. They're all drunks. They've got a bar down in the basement, hidden away, you know, and they go down there when they're not on nights and have a good booze-up.

"But blue watch are terrible, they like women. They're all married but they have women and girlfriends one way or another. They're notorious for orgies, you know. When they're having an orgy, you look over there at night and they've got a blue light up, a dark blue or dark red light up in the television room, and the curtains are half drawn. You hear noises coming from there, you know, music . . . and I have imagined myself there . . .

"Drinking plays a great deal to do with sex with me. When I've had a drink I just abandon myself and I really enjoy sex. I've gone for hours and hours, it releases everything. I become very sexually aggressive. I just make him lie there while I'm kissing him all over. I can only do that when I've had a drink, and he loves it.

"I never have fantasies with Bob. When we're fucking, I just don't need to, it's all there, it's so good, I suppose it's perfect. I can have so many orgasms and I can go on for hours and the next day I can't wait to do it again. I have fantasies about living together with Bob, about being free to make love all the time, anytime we want to. Sometimes we do it on the floor . . . or standing up. I quite like it standing up. It can be awkward so I stand on something.

"When I'm not with him I have fantasies about him, I can just be here in the house doing nothing and I see myself on a beach running through the sand and feeling the sun. The sky is all blue, and he comes towards me and he's so big, and he kisses me with his soft lips and it's all in the face – the tenderness, the love. And I can feel his hands on me – the way he touches me makes me feel so sexual – and I see us on the sand, in the water, his eyes like the colour of the sky. He touches my breasts; I can have an orgasm just by that. And we talk. Words, I like words when I make love. We talk about my hair, my back, things like that. I ask him if it's good, he tells me he loves me, and we make love on the sand, the waves rolling up over us occasionally. And we do all different positions and it goes on and on. I lie on my front and he comes in from the back, pulling me up against him, and we do it standing, kneeling, sitting . . .

"And then I think I would like to kill Harry, so that I might be free."

DIANAH

Dianah is a career woman: a film-maker who has directed and produced several documentaries for the BBC.

In her early thirties, she's not married, and tells me she's not particularly chasing a wedding ring, although inside her also dwells the romantic fantasy of happiness with Mr. Right.

Stylish in her dress from Ossie Clark, she served me with avocado and Dublin prawns accompanied with chilled white wine out of tall glasses she'd bought in Venice.

She was depressed the day I saw her – the BBC, after encouraging one of her projects had decided to cancel it. She talked about making her own film on sexual fantasies and said that ultimately she would like to use her own fantasies, as performance, but that in itself she thought was a fantasy as she hadn't the courage to do it; and anyway the family wouldn't stand for it. Her father is a lord and a politician. He has estates in Scotland and a mansion in the country, and a handful of apartments and houses in London.

She comes from a generation of rulers, Spartan upbringing, nannies with Victorian rule books under their starched aprons, and always dominant male figures – a patriarchal father, a brother at public school being prepared for his rule. The mother is of lesser consequence, often only a mouse to arrange dinner parties. It's no wonder that in Dianah's fantasy is the need to conquer and master dangerous situations.

She was given an elegant family flat in Hampstead, and this is where we meet. A huge four–poster wooden bed with canopies made of embroidered fringed shawls dominates the large white bedroom furnished to look Spanish.

She is extremely eloquent and sensitive, but seems to get distracted when speaking of her sexual fantasies, sometimes mumbling, difficult to understand, as though not wanting to be understood and perhaps compromised.

****

"I'd like to ask you what the women you've been interviewing have been talking about. Where they visual things, were they romantic things? Because what I'd really like to do is do this film. My opinion is that there ought to be more women's sexual fantasy films. I'd like to be able to do my own . . . but I tend to veer towards the classical. I mean anyone I've talked to about it is so much more interested in that than anything else. It's a totally unexplored area. It's stupid to waste all your energy making a film about children moving from one school to another, or something, when there's a real need for a film in this area.

"The only thing that men think woman have fantasies about is about big pricks . . . and it's totally untrue.

"It's very interesting that men really do like porn and women don't. But men really like it and go to extremes to get it . . . some men, anyway.

"First of all it's really to do with cocks and not really to do with cunts, and even if it was to do with cunts it's not really beautifully done, is it? You don't feel . . . most of the attitudes, the sort of perverted attitudes of women are always really available, and men are always the masters. And then it's badly filmed or photographed, and then it's totally unconvincing and not up to the standard one requires.

"All the men think about whips. I don't find that terribly sexy, really. I'd like to make women's pornography which would be very beautiful and romantic. I sort of think of the classics in pornographic terms. For instance, Ferdinand, that children's story – the bull. He would be sitting under a tree and then he and the matador would stand in the middle of the ring and not fight, because they wanted to fuck.

"I think a lot can be done, but of course it means finding the money – someone to back you.

"On the whole I think there should be more well done pornography and beautiful sex . . . one would turn on much more. Pornography is a horrible word . . . the trouble is it's quite easy to define pornography, but it's less easy to define obscenity. They just sort of get them mixed up and lump them together. I think it would be lovely to readdress the balance by just showing them how beautiful it can be . . .

"I don't know whether it is because of my father, who had always been such an incredible problem, so dominating, but I never . . . had an orgasm with a man and I didn't fuck at all until I was twenty-six, because I was so inhibited, and I went through the whole of my Oxford years without it.

"But I think that orgasms are . . . I mean when I do have them it's fantastic, and of course it bothers me like hell that I don't have them more often; you see I have such an irregular sex life. I'm so inhibited, I don't sort of fuck around.

"I did, before I went to America. I went out with people who were my father–image, you know. They were powerful, achieving, famous people. I had various relationships, sort of six months each, a year or something, and they were totally unsuitable men who just bored me really; and then finally the last one left me and I started going out with God knows who, and then in sixteen nights I had sixteen different men, all the same, all known or something: journalists, writers, music. I felt so . . . I just sort of went crazy, that's when I left and I didn't sleep with another man for about a year at least, because I was just through with it.

"And I also stayed in a house by myself for a month. I went pretty berserk. It was a very wet summer in Connecticut, but I did regain something . . .

"My father had always been so frightfully ambitious for us. He wanted us all to be Prime Ministers no less, and therefore you have to go through this, all the time, this frightful thing, this principle. You have to be doing something which has a label, a name or something. And my brothers are all very powerful you know . . . politically, except the youngest one opted out and he's a poet, you know. He's wildly attractive – if he walks into the room there's something about him: he's got beautiful black eyes and a wonderful manner and he rides horses so well and you wouldn't think that he was anything to do with Eton at all.

"My father is so awful, he just always says you're a dismal failure; you've been a poet for six years and you're a complete failure, so why don't you do something else?

"He's the most turned on and the most attractive . . . I'd love to fuck him . . . I haven't . . . but I would. He came in here one day and said, I think incest . . . I think incest is out, but I think we ought to live together, you and me, my sister, so we can work out our relationship.

"I said I wasn't thinking about incest at that moment . . . and the thing is, he does think about it a lot. He's got into bed with me, and we haven't fucked because . . . because of the taboos really, and because it is too delicate . . . but that was a long time ago. But now I wouldn't, because I know it would screw him up even more than he is, you know.

"But I had this incredible fantasy about him once, this incredible orgasm and beautiful fantasy . . . going parachute jumping . . . once . . . to prove to my father.

"The instructor lined us up, six men and me. He told us to put the parachutes on. We did. I was absolutely horrified because I thought, well for God's sake he'll show us what to do and he didn't, not until the last minute when I had visions of the parachute coming apart even before it opened.

"And then I got into the plane. He said, you just sit on the edge of the plane, on the side; you just sit there and you fall out forward, and put your arms out like that. There were six men with very brown skins, curly hair, pressing against me, so I was right behind the pilot.

"And the first parachute was pushed over the side and you saw it disappearing and you longed to see where it was so you could make some idea of where you were going to be when you jumped. And there you are in the belly of the plane . . . and the wind went up your trouser leg . . . wheeee . . . and it is very cold but it was hot, hot, hot outside, and it was about six o'clock at night . . . and it was time. Finally each one jumped out separately and I had to jump out last.

"You desperately want to pull your legs away and pull your legs in again and just look out and think about eternal space just between the earth and the sky. And I thought I'd never be able to do it and they'd be right, and it was impossible being so frightened, and then suddenly he tapped me on the shoulder, and that made me fall out and I put my arms out like they said and then suddenly the parachute opened and I got this terrific drag and then I began to laugh and cry and then it was incredibly sexy because the whole world . . . the whole world is out there . . . you're coming down, soft, white, fluffy and it's absolutely beautiful. Very slow . . . and I never looked up. I never saw the parachute above me . . . which is a pity. Someone said it must have been there . . . and I felt more alive than I felt at any moment before or since, because your pulse is rushing and your whole being is stretched.

"I remember that my head went into movies . . . into images. But just visual, no thought going through . . . all very sort of beautiful . . . quite cutting and kaleidoscopic and Elysian. And then it was . . . I am stretched out on satin sky-blue sheets, and the man is stroking me, tying me with silk threads, very, very gently to the posts, and I see his hips, the rhythm in the way he moves around, walking all the way around the bed. The bed is like a love machine: there are knobs, and he's dialling all of them and the right things are coming to me . . . and I look into my brother's eyes . . . beyond the dark irises . . . beyond the sky into the stars . . . forever. And then I become some sort of molecular . . . things passing through my head . . . things you feel in touch with all the time . . . in touch with the universe . . . the family of man. I feel at the moment, at the moment of coming, terribly aware of life . . . it comes streaming through . . . and my brother says to me, sister, the reason why we haven't met our match is because our match is each other."

DONNA

In billowing skirt of deep colours she sits softly on a low bed in a drab room: her life surrounding her. The television on from early afternoon is mostly unseen by her large, kohl framed black like eyes. An ironing board is leaning against a dull wall and a pile of washing crowd a corner. A smiling boy of three is wholly involved in the ticking of a yellow clock; a pretty little girl, who looks just like her pretty mother, is reading; boy of ten getting ready to spend the weekend with his father, is spilling bread crumbs on the carpet with the holes.

When she speaks she's the actress: delicately tilting her head, lowering her large eyes, waving long finger . . . pausing for effect.

Too gentle to battle for success, her career is unimpressive. Moving with the changes, impermanent, she's lived with several men, had their children, and then left them. She lives mostly thanks to the Social Security check given to her by the state.

Doe-like, sensitive, fine featured, delicate, gentle, but when Donna loses her temper she breaks everything in sight.

****

"When I'm making love I become a fourteen year old . . . well I do. Like you've got three kids and you're with somebody new and they're younger than you and they would like to wipe out your children, in a way, but they know they can't so they say, I'd like to have met you when you were much younger and when you didn't have all your complications and things, and all your other different men that are obviously . . . like the fathers of your children are always going to stay throughout your life. I've got three different men who are always going to stay with me, so it's almost an impossible situation to create a new relationship . . . well not impossible . . . it's hard. So sometimes I've got to pretend when I'm making love that I'm fourteen.

"I lay the whole trip on the other person too. I start off by saying, what were you doing when you were fourteen? Were you at school, can you remember the summer holidays, was it this, was it that? And make people just drop into it.

"And you're already sexually aware of each other because you're naked and snuggling and suddenly you find you're becoming two young children.

"When you're fourteen years old you're very shy or you can be a very wild fourteen-year-old, you don't care.

"I become very nervous, you know, like the first time, when you've never actually been to bed with somebody and then you're in bed and actually can't do it because you've never done it before, and you jump up and grab your clothes and say, I'm still a virgin. So it almost ends up . . . I develop the situation so strongly, because I can make people go through it, that I've actually ended up by practically getting raped.

"Well I would like to get raped so that I don't have to make that awful decision . . ."

ELIZABETH

It was raining. Elizabeth came round after work, freezing in hot pants. I said I though she ought to be wearing something warmer. She answered that all the girls at the office wore them and besides she had a date (blind) with a film producer and he'd probably take her somewhere 'in'. "Well that would certainly be warmer than somewhere 'out'," I remarked and we both laughed.

Her platinum hair is coiffed in a bouffant hairdo, and soft false lashes encircle sparkling, if confused, vivid blue eyes. A large sloppy mouth features prominently in a very pretty, doll-like, pale face.

Her body is round – she believes in three solid meals daily; takes amphetamines to keep from getting over hungry; they make her speedy, contradicting her natural laziness.

She's generous, never bitchy, warm, helpful, charming with children.

Born is South Africa, she left school before the final exams, trained as a secretary and has been living in England for six years now. At present she works as secretary to a film star (she's a movie star groupie) earning thirty pound a week (before tax) and shares a flat in Knightsbridge with two girlfriends.

She's prone to depression, is a-political, aggressive sexually; is overwhelmed by 'names', has orgasms with ease and loves orgies.

She is also an avid reader, reads several books simultaneously, but never finishing any; and speaks eloquently, quickly and forcefully to give the impression that she's in control.

She drinks heavily to the extent of passing out, is addicted to the cinema, loves television (indiscriminately), is honest, gutsy and a loyal friend.

At twenty-seven she has never had an affair which has lasted longer than a month and tells me she prefers one-night-stands.

****

"I'm very shy, I find everything difficult, and probably I overcompensate. Sometimes I feel I'm being rather heavy, I talk a lot in my nervousness – and I'm always very chatty. That's when I hate myself, the Miss Personality bit, because I'm basically very quiet.

"I'm frightened of insecurity – I don't think that means financially – but I'm getting older now and I'm wondering what I'm going to do . . . where I'm going to go. I feel that I'm losing contact. My family is not the same anymore, I've been away too long. I know it's there, but it's not close.

"I don't think I'm going to get married. I never know if it's me or them. I guess it's me, but I've never been able to keep a man. I get bored or terrified. Actually I do run away. I run. You know all of a sudden I won't answer the phone; I'm terrified. I'd like the security of a relationship, but not the bondage.

"Shirley McLain's got the right idea: her husband is in Tokyo, she flies through and spends some time with him, and then away again.

"I don't really need that much sex – three or four times a week is the most – but if I get a lot I want more and more. Young boys; I love making love with young boys. I'm always much more relaxed on the first night than I am any other time. I'm like a shy little girl the second time. I suppose the first time's an act. I just go in there as bold as brass. I mean, I say, where's the bedroom? You know, if I see a guy who's shy, I laugh at his insecurity.

"In bed I'm on top, I'm the one doing it, I'm fucking him. That's very important, not to feel that men only want you because they're fucking you.

"But the second time around it gets more complicated because then you're more down to earth, you know him, you've been there. It's almost a bore, the second time. I suppose the fantasy that you're conquering is no longer there. Also you must remember there's always the feeling of the unknown that's very exciting. I mean the feeling of wanting someone is almost more exciting than the actual having.

"I never pull a girl though, they pull me. Except apparently I made a pass at a boyfriend's fifteen-year-old daughter, but I didn't know it was his daughter. Oh wow! Some girls I really fancy but I don't make a pass at them. I'd be too terrified in case they thought I was butch, you know. Frightened of being labelled a dyke, in case I made the wrong move – so I usually wait for them to come to me. And let's face it, if you're in London long enough you get propositioned. And usually I'm lying on top of them too, and I like to make love to their bodies because each time it's so unique.

"You know you have so many men . . . but the difference . . . you know to compare the two is so incredible. Well you know, don't you? I think everyone should have one of their own sex. The delicate hands, and all here, round the shoulders, the soft lips . . . and the breasts, and the body and cunt. You know I wasn't aware of this bone here – the mound – till I went down on a girl. Now I'm very aware of the actual structure of the pelvis. Incredible. And it's very clean too. I always thought it would be messy, but you see, as you suck the juices go in anyway and it's not that sloppy.

"I can't bear a man to come in my mouth and usually, if I feel the time is right, I mention the fact. Please don't come in my mouth, I'll say. Ugh, wow! Awful.

"There's hardly any taste to a woman, but I suppose I was pissed at the time, so I couldn't tell the taste. That's another thing, I never . . . I don't know if I could now – probably – but I have never had a scene without drinking or smoking pot.

"And I like a girl to go down on me . . . that feeling . . . that softness. I hold her head in my hands, here, you know, holding her but not pushing her. I love to feel her long hair. Some people don't know how to go down on you, some men, oh! Some of them are ferocious and then I can't enjoy it. I have images of my clit disappearing down some guy's throat . . . forever and ever. Oh, that would be awful.

"I never have fantasies when I'm fucking. I'm so aware of everything when I'm fucking, I'm surprised I come at all. I'm aware of every tiny detail: the feeling of the skin, the walls around me, him, me, my breathing, my reaction, my cunt . . . whatever's happening. In the end I have to force myself to relax to come.

"I feel myself relaxing right through when I'm going to come. Like it's a melting feeling, and then when you come, it's just like dying. That's what it is about orgies – so full, so much happening at once, everything going on.

"I have fantasies only when I'm masturbating. I was very young when I first discovered masturbation. When I was a kid I didn't know what sex was about. I didn't have a name for masturbation, but I knew I was doing something naughty. I don't know how – nobody ever told me – but I had the feeling that I shouldn't tell anyone and I mustn't be caught doing it, or tell any one what I was thinking.

"I masturbate like this, just my legs crossed tightly. I don't put my fingers there at all . . . just press my thighs   together . . . and think dirty. I don't like touching myself, apart from the *Pifco*[1], and with that I don't really have to fantasize that much, you know – that lasts fifteen seconds.

---

[1] A brand of electric vibrator.

"The fantasies got more elaborate because I hate using the same ones. I have to change them all the time. I'll have variations on a theme, but never the same one. This one I had a few days ago . . .

"I'm in a big hall, in Roman times – huge feasts, elaborate meats, fruits, wines, orgies. There's a big fat man on a raised chair – bold, and glistening with oil. And he never spoke, never said a word. And there's a woman on a throne next to him, enormous like her consort, and all these semi-nude people around them. Like a Fellini movie, *Satyricon*. Beautiful people, yet obscene – scattered around on couches, cushions; women with their breasts out, transparent chiffon dresses, men very drunk, bawdy.

"The bald fat man sitting there had his cock on a little purple velvet cushion sticking in front of him, with his legs apart. And all the women had to take turns at sucking his cock before the game started. And the woman on the throne had men all around her, touching her, rubbing grapes on her, playing with her cunt.

"You could sit anywhere you wanted to. I was sitting next to a woman and I was innocent, unaware that she would make any advances or anything like that. And then the big spectacle began.

"They had people rolling on the floor, acrobats, dancers, all fucking at the end as part of the act. And for the finale they bring in this huge cage complex. It was set up like a house and in it there was a condemned woman. By way of reprieve, if she survived the act she would be set free. She was nude except for an apron, and she was cleaning the house waiting for her husband. And they let in this huge gorilla wearing a little bolero to make him look like the man of the house; and then she, frantic to have him, to get it over with, would set him down (he was partly trained) and he would sit at the table in the caged house and she would serve him his food. And naturally the gorilla would break and drop things because he was a gorilla – although partly trained. And finally she would have to get him excited, and she did really desperately try, as her life depended on it.

"I would sit watching her, feeling her anxiety, as she would grab his cock, masturbate it, suck it; but he wouldn't take any notice. And she would go on and on sucking and finally she would get through to him, managing to get his cock going. And in the mean time the woman next to me has rolled over and has her hand on my cunt. She tickles me, and the gorilla starts fucking the woman with fury, quickly, quickly. She screams in agony and he crushes her to death, and the whole hall would be fucking by now, and then this woman would go down on me, and that's how I'd come.

FIORE

Fiore is a sex-goddess.

Born in a village in the Italian Alps into a family of numerous brothers and sisters, she recalls a happy childhood. Her father, now retired, was the local butcher.

When she was seventeen she went to Florence on an art scholarship. At nineteen, a virgin, she was married to a young photographer whom she divorced eleven years later, when, after many rows and separations, her husband, who neither satisfied her obsessive sexuality nor her affectionate, warm nature, ran away with their maid.

In her early thirties, she looks much younger, with raven hair down her back and big oval bosoms which are her pride.

She designs Voguish clothes, works only when she needs money; is extravagant, spends generously on others; lives in a luxuriously furnished two-room apartment overlooking the Seine.

The outfits she creates for herself are provocative, emphasizing her round sexy body. Her face, bosoms, and curves, make constant reference to sexuality. Fucking is the habit, the drug.

Because of her good looks, charm and easy ways, she's one of the darlings in the high-class, high-moneyed international society. She enjoys being with the rich and beautiful. Goes to parties with renegade Italian princes and Salvador Dali; has threesomes with jet-set couples; spends summers in villas in St. Tropez and receives pricey gifts from lovers. Once, for a birthday present, a member of the French government gave her a whore from a highly prized Parisian brothel.

Energetic, she lives each day for what it is: loving it, getting the most out of it. She's relentlessly flirtatious, lacks a sense of humour, writes poetry and becomes very though when circumstances require it. She worships cats, wondering off into the night to feed strays, and truly finds it difficult to believe that ugly women get lovers.

She says she'll not get married again, likes living on her own; yet she is a home-maker: entertains lavishly, is a Cordon Bleu cook and has many friends – retaining relationships and affections for years, and has fallen in love, more than once, with gigolos.

When I interviewed her she was in London to find Dan, the young lover who obsesses her, and who, of late, hasn't been over available to her.

****

"I never have fantasies when I fuck, you know, but I love it when a man uses them. Like, if he could tell me he's fucking a beautiful girl with big tits, and he'd fuck her and I'd fuck her – oh it excites me so much to hear a man talk to me. That's what I love most.

"But I don't have so many sexual fantasies anymore. I had many of them when I was younger, before I really knew how to come. I had the most incredible dreams . . . I dreamt once I made love to 100 monkeys. They raped me and raped my husband. They took him away and I was laying there in the grass on the hill, with hundreds of monkeys and two big monkeys just held me, all of them fucked me and I was very ashamed to realize that I loved it. And then when I woke up I felt guilty about having this dream, because I enjoyed it so much . . . all those monkeys!!!

"But now of course, all I want is a man like Dan. There's nothing I really want anymore, you know, since I've known him. With him, I would do anything with him. I like to do everything with a man; it's a lovely situation, I think . . . to do everything. But when I think of anything it's always with him, you know, I don't think of myself anymore.

"He turns me even more onto fantasies than anybody else because he was so much against them, but I could feel inside he wanted it as bad as me. I knew he has a lot of fantasies but he was never free enough to tell me about it. He thought I wanted him pure and I thought he wanted me pure, so we were very, very shy about each other's things. Only on our last acid trip we both admitted how much we really liked things happening – at least in our minds to play with . . .

"I'm very strange, I don't really need sex all that much at all. I'm just very happy to lie and think about something. I'm like that. The thought of Dan already will last me the rest of my life. I know I will never forget him; he gave me too many things. Like music . . . he made me listen. He made me really feel. He made me like absolutely everything, you know. That's what I think he's valuable for . . . for being alive.

"There's something about this . . . I don't know, it can't be love, because there wouldn't be so much pain involved. But what is it that's between him and me? It's not just sexual, you know. Sometimes we meet on very strange levels, but he's is always higher than mine.

"He's just such a man, you know. How could I tell you how good he is? He just knows every minute, every hour of the day how to take me. It's never the same, you know, every time it's different, and so perfect, so pure. I've never had anything like him before, never in my life. He makes you a slave and on the other hand he makes you a chief, you know, he makes you both . . . it's . . . so incredible.

"Making love he just stops, and he looks at me, and if I try to face away or try to put my eyes down, he makes me look at him, because he knows I'm always scared of love. I'm always scared of lovemaking; I always was scared of it, and I still am, and he would very much like to get me rid of that.

"He said once that he just wants me to be completely free. That's why I walk with my shoulders hunched, he thinks, because I'm not completely free . . . there's something . . . a block somewhere.

"He's been with many famous women, you know. He was with Mama Cass, you know, who is a very fat lady. But then he was with such beautiful women . . . and sure they all like him, and he hates the fact that he is a good lover. He hates to make love, really. He always says that it takes all the energy from him.

"Everybody always said I was all the time so sexy and I never really was, you know; I just looked like that. I was sexy, I mean I like to make love . . . but I certainly never knew anything about it, until I met him. And he tells me how fat I am and it makes me so hurt.

"I was a virgin when I got married, and I never came with my husband once. I never knew that, you see . . . I always thought that that was coming, what I did, and it never was. A girlfriend once said something about clitoris. I said, what is it, and she said, you know, where you caress yourself. I said, I don't caress myself, and she said, come on, and she showed me where it was. And so I went home and I did it and it was so beautiful and the strange thing was, I should have known then that there was something wrong with my love life; but I was so amorous with my husband that I didn't want to admit it . . . not until much later, and I never had the heart to tell him. So I playacted and the idiot never knew I never came.

"And then I stated to have lovers and I couldn't come either, and then I had an English Lord who was the first man who allowed me to be completely free. This is why I thought I loved him, I suppose, because he was a fantastic lover. He was very perverted, but I loved it, you know, it turned me on. He let me do things. I always dreamed of caressing myself while I made love and things like that. And he encouraged me . . . and he liked to watch me masturbate.

"And then I started to do it with girls. I just love to do it to them so much – that turns me on so much I come very easily afterwards.

"The other night, you know, it happened in Paris. It was so, beautiful – the bell rang and this couple said, oh you know, somebody just sent us from Spain, and could we sleep here this night? And I said, you know, I've been alone in my apartment for two months and that's how I like it, but you might as well come in, but only for one night.

"The boy was very nice, he was writing poems all the time and playing his guitar – and the girl was always looking at me like that, and I thought, why not? And I poured hot water in the pool on the terrace, with lots of bubbles, and I said, why don't we have a bath? So we all had a bath, and Jesus, what a night . . . till seven o'clock in the morning. I never had a girl like that before in my life.

"I was the first woman she'd ever had. I didn't even do much to her but . . . I've never seen a girl who wants to be fucked that much. I was completely worn out and dead and exhausted, and she just started again. She's eighteen, you know, a dancer, a very beautiful body and . . . a lovely girl, and we never said a word, we never talked once, I never knew her name.

"I'd love to see Dan make love to boys . . . I'd adore that. I did see that once – I saw a boy fuck a boy, and suck him off at the same time. He had his cock in the back and he was bent completely and he sucked him off. I men what more do you want; I mean why does a man want a woman if he has that? It was very beautiful to look at; it turned me on so much.

"Dan doesn't like the idea that I think he's a little queer. He's done it, but no in front of me. But I love the idea of him doing it, and I love the idea too that he beats them up a little afterwards. He gets furious after he does it and then he beats them up. But they love it. And I sometimes wish . . . well, he didn't really beat me up too much, but he gave me a slap.

"I never like to be beaten, but with him it was different . . . it just fitted. But he seems much less aggressive now. I don't think he would probably beat me again, you know, he's sort of worked that out. I think his anger . . . most of it . . . is just sadness now.

"I want so much to be able to fuck him. I want that a cock grows on me; that's my biggest dream. And he would like me to do it so badly. But I guess I'll never have one. He wants me to buy one, and I'm too shy to go into a shop and buy one, and anyway I hate the idea of artificial cocks so badly. But I guess I'll have to get friendly with one because that's what he wants me to do.

"He's the first man who's ever done it to me in the back; and that's so fantastic. I once asked my husband to do it and he said, are you crazy, it stinks there, and I felt such a whore. But now with Dan . . . we do it all the time, till I'm an open wound and I have to see a doctor and the doctor said, who on earth has done that to you? So much . . . all day . . . all night . . . it hurt me so terribly I had to stop.

"And he came all the time . . . always hard. I think it's the most beautiful cock, so beautiful, so strong. He doesn't just go in me, he really goes into me, you know, with his eyes and everything. It's just like I have the whole of him inside me when he's inside me. I love to think he's as big as a house. Very often when we make love his cock is like a sabre . . . I would love it to cut me in two. And he can fuck and come, you know – I hate the man who doesn't come – and then he makes it go right on and on . . ."

GILLIAN

Born in New York, Gillian is a sophisticated, well travelled young woman in her late twenties, at present sojourning in London.

She lives in an expensive modern apartment block with a view, where ageing doormen in black uniforms silently point impersonal directions down thickly carpeted passageways.

There's an air of opulence in her flat: expensive works of art, gilded fixtures, and Persian carpets. The elegance is genuine; the colours are rich, matte, deep.

Stacks of books are neatly placed in polished wooden shelves and on coffee tables: art, travel, poetry; expensively bound volumes, glossy magazines, accepted erotic art. A collection of rock and roll records and Bach.

She wears nineteen-thirty clothes which suit her petit frame perfectly, and wedge heeled shoes that show off neat ankles. Her blonde hair, cropped stylishly by Vidal Sassoon, frames a pale face with flawless skin. Above her sparkling, inquisitive, clairvoyant, grey eyes are shapely pencilled lashes; her full lips are generously painted with, as she puts it, whore-red lipstick.

She's cryptic, witty, cynical and warm; frequents an expensive fortune teller and is seriously involved with astrology. An accomplished pianist she wants to be a song writer, and her ready laugh, even when she laughs at herself, is catchy.

Over a glass of chilled white wine she tells me her imaginative fantasies and funny stories with confidence and eloquence; and is aware that because of her background and because she's an aesthete she can only be in love with perfection, and the easiest way for her to have this is to crate it in her mind.

****

"Why I want to talk about fantasies is because mine are so strong – not that they are necessarily sexual, but they are so strong they rule me from any real relationship, because the relationship becomes what I think the guy is, and he isn't; and I'd invent these things about people so that I could justify going to bed with them. Like I have a huge, huge fantasy and it helps, because if you don't have any emotions, if you don't give yourself any emotions about it, you start really noticing . . . spots on his back, and . . . vulgar words, not vulgar words when you're fucking , but just kind of general vulgar word in conversation.

"But if I make up a fantasy about somebody, you know — you know, love is blind — a euphemism for fantasy. And fantasies blind you, and you become blind inside the fantasy.

"I've had fantasies from a very young age. It's funny because they are kind of male chauvinist fantasies. When I was six, so that's over twenty years ago now, we were living in Rome, and I remember lying in this bed that had a canopy on top of it and wishing, praying God that I would have big breasts; and really praying, praying and getting terribly turned on thinking about it, and then it got worse because my imagination got carried away with me and I imagined getting bigger and bigger and bigger.

"Two years later I was having fantasies about being in hell with about four hundred other women, seeing myself much older, with huge breasts, going down to about here . . . and devils with pitchforks sort of hurling at us . . . sort of putting their pitchforks into our breasts, pricking them.

"It was a pretty vivid scene. There was fire, you could hear the fire, and the devils were all skinny and black, with long, black pointed tails at the back and horns in the front. And the women were all sort of the same, tall and rather fat; with big bottoms and big, long, droopy breasts. That was for sticking the pitchfork into.

"And while I was fantasizing, what I used to do was take a hair out of my head — I had very long hair then — and hold either end of it, and put it between my legs. I didn't quite know what there was between my legs, but I knew that it felt kind of strange if you rubbed this one little hair back and forth.

"Well, the funny thing is that when I started to get hair down there I stopped doing it, because it was kind like poetic justice, you know, I'd been doing this thing with the hair and suddenly I was getting hairs there.

"We were living in this peculiar situation in Rome, because my mother's parents lived with us too, and my grandmother was always trying to control my life. I was her only grandchild that she really liked — all the others were in America. And she kept on thinking I was going to die, and she was always banging her nose into my life, and maybe there was just something about her physical presence, which was fat, and she had the kind of breasts in the devil dream that influenced me a lot.

"They all lead a very superficial existence. But you know, like it wasn't that kind of household where my father read Playboy or my mother was always going for a drink — nothing like that. There was never any opening up into the deep currents that I suppose you sometimes have in families, and I never had it in mine you know. Never an intimation that there was such a thing as sex.

"At eleven I started going to Ireland, to stay with some people who were even more aesthetic but much looser about life than my parents were, and everything got on a completely different plane. I started having fantasies about certain people who were also staying at the house. There were kind of . . . horses, and the horses would go to stud, or whatever it's called, in front of the windows, and I'd watch this girl watching the horses. I'd lie in bed imagining that there was a whole bunch of women, again always the mass of women, you know, a lot of them, lined up, like the mares of hell. We were all on this big wheel . . . big, flat wheels . . . we were practically crucified on them, and this huge man coming up . . .

"I had my first kind of sexual experience when I was sixteen . . . and it wasn't fucking, but it was everything but. And I didn't enjoy it, even though I was absolutely in love with the guy. I mean, I'll never love anybody so much, but what he wanted was completely different from what I wanted. I wanted poems, walks, and really wispy things like that; which I think was influenced by this semi-artistic upbringing that I've had. Yes, and the sea . . .

"Like the first time I was kissed was in a horrible nightclub called *Kit Kat* in Rome. He leaped on me, banged my head on the wall, and started kissing me, and I was just sixteen. I went home and wrote on this piece of paper that I've still got somewhere, about how one's first kiss shouldn't be like that: you should be naked, under heavy woollen capes on the seashore at dawn. I . . . I mean it was really essential, because I was really imagining the walk, and the fields . . .

" I'm always more sensual than sexual in fact, because, like this guy really screwed up when I was so young, by playing around with me when I was only in love with him and didn't understand the whole sex thing. He tried, I suppose three times, to make love to me, and I really wanted to, I wanted to give myself to him, but I wasn't quite sure what to do with my arms and legs and I couldn't understand why he was trembling, and so he said – he phoned me up one day and said, look, it never happened. And from then I went into a complete Victorian decline.

"I remember one day in a shop I saw a shirt, which was the kind of shirt he wore – it was rough wool, tartan – and I went up to it and I just put my cheek against it and started to relive the times, all the times we'd been together, but the feeling of it, and not only the sensual feeling, but what my emotions had been . . . because . . . again . . . my ideas are so different from dreams, because every bit of emotion is so bloody important. I can create emotion; I can do it by having a fantasy about somebody. Like . . . if I like a certain guy I have fantasies about him. I went on this skiing holiday when I was seventeen, and I had fantasies at night about my skiing instructor and that's when I started to masturbate. And on the next day, on the slopes, I couldn't bear looking at him in the face . . . because of all these things I'd be thinking, you know, and like, oh, about him being in bed with me, touching my body . . .

"I've only slept with about fifteen people, which I don't think is a lot. None of them I've really lived with for a long time. They've all been very short things and the longest, in Rome, was the most unsatisfying. It was really, really horrible, oh, that's when we got into a fantasy trip, I mean the guy wanted me to be . . . like a little girl, and when we fucked, it was like he was raping me . . . which the first time I thought was very groovy, because I'd never been able to even admit a fantasy to anybody before, but it turned out that every time I had to do that it wasn't so funny anymore. In fact it was a great big bore. And he was English and had all these problems about his father and he always wanted me to masturbate.

" I have a thing about masturbating . . . when I've finished I'm really furious, because it's just me . . . and it just makes me hornier, and it makes me mad that I can't go out, just meet somebody and say, let's fuck, instead of pretending I was fucking someone. It's so ludicrous: you're just agitating your pelvis against the mattress or against thin air . . . and your hands down there . . . you know damn well that it's *your* fingers.

"I have sort of two opposite kinds of fantasies, because I have one fantasy about being terribly, terribly passive, maybe you know with several different men, which I've never done. I mean, I've only like fucked one man at the time. And then there's another one, of being much more active than the man, and doing things to him which I usually can't do. I mean, I hate fucking men , I mean, sometimes I do it if I'm really carried away, but I really don't like it . . . but I have certain fantasies about really enjoying it . . . but then when it comes to it, there's a kind of block.

"I suppose I'm really masochistic. There was this male chauvinist American that I met at a dinner party. I mean he's this pretty unattractive guy with crinkly, horrible, balding hair and jowls: a really ugly face with pale washed-out eyes. And we're talking quite naturally and he's quite witty and then offers to drive me home and in the car he takes my hand and puts it on his prick, and he says, touch me and I say no, and I took my hand away. And then he said, you're coming back to my place, and we're in the car going on the highway back to New York and I said no, I'm not going back to your place, and he said, yes you are, or I shall let you out here; so I said okay, I'll go to your place.

"So we went back to his place and his bedroom was really horrible . . . there was a bed in the middle, and a very loud air-conditioner . . . the bed that wasn't wide enough, and he was very tall and rather fat, and ugly as hell. Huge, white, flabby body, and so he said, undress, so I undressed, and he undressed. And he got into bed, and he immediately made a kind of hole in it, because it's very springy. I roll over, so we start fucking, and I was just trying to disassociate, trying to imagine that the lower part of my body was made independently – it was the only thing he was paying attention to anyway.   He was kissing my anus, and afterwards when he finished he said, hey, you're not a bad little lay.

"I felt so demeaned by him talking to me like that, after we'd been fucking, and then he said, suck me, and I said no, and he said suck me, and instead of saying oh shit, I burst into tears, and I explained that I didn't like it, and I wasn't going to do it, and he tried to force me and I got even more upset.

"But instead of leaving, because I really dug being humiliated – this is what is so disgusting – I stayed there all night, and I couldn't sleep all night because there was this air-conditioner, and there was this hole in the bed that kept rolling towards his body, and I kept on gripping onto the bed, and in the morning I thought, right, keep your head together, take a bath and go, and you'll never have to see him again.

"So anyway, I leap off the bed and I go into the bathroom and I'm running the water, thinking, wash yourself, wash yourself, everything will be okay and he suddenly leaps into the bathroom and he says, you bitch! I leaped up and I said, what have I done, what is it now? And he says, I was supposed to have the first bath!!!! But really furious.

"Then there was another one who was fucking a well known socialite at the same time. He kept on phoning her up, while we were in bed, and saying, you know, Hi C., when are you giving your ball? And his incitement for me to sleep was to say, look, Porthault sheets. You know Porthault sheets are the most expensive sheets you can buy in New York. And he was really the mechanical American woman-fucker that would, you know, heave away with his hips in one way for a while and then he'd sort of change a leg and give the same amount of time to the other way of doing it, then do another change of position and keep coming out with these remarks like, hey, you're really a cute little thing, which . . . is so horrible. And those were the things that made me not want to see him again. You know, all those little unconscious put-downs, of like trying to please a real imbecile . . . right, 'you cute little thing' suck my cock.' I mean, are there women who go around pulling up their skirts and saying, suck me?

" I mean, maybe that's what should happen with woman's lib, but I mean, I think it's so horrid when a man takes his thing out and just announces . . . even in the kitchen: 'suck me'. Never ever worried that it might smell of piss. I've had it suggested to me. What an assumption that you'd only be interested in that, or that it's the thing they're proudest of in fact, and if they're really together about their bodies, great, but if it's sort of peeping out between two folds of cashmere trousers that cost 200 quid, and you've got to get down on your knees, it's really horrible.

"My fantasy, in fact, was I felt like getting down there and biting it off."

GWEN

Gwen invites me to lunch. She feels uninhibited, she says, is interested in discussing her fantasies – as long as names weren't mentioned. "My parents-in-law would have a seizure – which might not be a bad thing at that!" she adds laughing.

Fragile young woman: a mass of black hair and prominent, round breasts. Delicate, beautiful face, she looks much younger than her 28 years. But then I notice brush-strokes of pain in her pastel blue yes.

The aura projected in the dark, heavy, two-room apartment is one of melancholy. Except for the Ajax-sparkling kitchen – where she produces a skyscraper soufflé – the place is chaos. Week-old newspapers amongst fading flowers in ceramic vases; ashtrays emptied out in the pretty fireplace; dust; windowpanes made opaque by months of grey, city grime. She likes things clean and tidy, she affirms, yet laziness dominates: "I detest housework!"

Although they are always broke she doesn't want a job from nine to five. "Can't type or do shorthand, and earning ten quid a week as a shop assistant hardly seems worth it."

The difficulty with getting out of bed in the morning is a source of constant guilt: "I need ten hours sleep. I guess I'm into dreaming. It's escapism, I know."

Her musical voice is impregnated with childish tones, and she uses a nice smile to charm my attention away from her self-consciousness. At all times, like a cat, she studies me feeling her.

"My father was a farmer. We had a lovely place in Wales. Rambling cottage surrounded by mauve mountains, lots of animals. He drank, was violent, mistreated my mother – not too an unusual story, I suppose. Anyway I loved him . . . and he me. He killed himself, and I came to London. My husband is very much like him – drinks too. One repeats the pattern, doesn't one? He loves me very much, though. My husband, I mean.

That the four year childless marriage is a failure is something she doesn't admit; blaming lack of money for their difficulties. Deluding herself that tomorrow things will fall into place, she stays with him, out of habit, a need for the security of the familiar.

They have sex four times a week, always at her husband's instigation. "The one time I won't do it is in the morning," she says with determination.

****

"I'm frightened of men – physically I mean. But then I'm a coward. Sometimes I think I'm a lesbian . . . except I've never been in love with a woman as I have been with men. I like women, though and I've been to bed with them sometime. I like to spend time with them, I feel familiar with them. I believe homosexuality is the truest relationship . . . we're on the same mental wavelength with our own sex.

"I've never had a proper orgasm . . . I mean with him inside me. I think perhaps I don't like fucking itself . . . I mean I don't like my husband's penis inside me. He's rather large, it hurts me. The moment he starts to penetrate I become dry. The pain is dreadful . . . piercing. He's always accusing me of being dry. I try to make him come in other ways . . . I mean I have to make him come in other ways. He likes stories of things I've done or would like to do. He always makes me come; violent, short orgasms . . . like a wave that sweeps over me with great force, then drowns me. I never want to go on after I've come. I can't. It revolts me. So I hold back. I could come immediately – as soon as he touches my breasts. They're very sensitive. He knows the amount of pressure I need. I need force – he knows that. Maybe I'm a masochist. I don't really like to make it with my husband – not that I make it with anyone else – yet he makes me come every time. I hate to always have to invent stories, always having to think instead of feeling. But then I get involved in my fantasy . . .

"We walk in the park, the grass is pastel, heavy branches of huge trees shade us from the brilliant sun. We find a girl . . . young . . . twelve . . . fourteen . . . innocent . . . beautiful. We talk with her, make friends, bring her back here, give her tea relax her; involve her in us, in him. He touches her a little. Her bare arms, her long, soft hair. She's shy, very attracted to him, excited by her feelings, her giddiness, the way he looks at her. I say I have to go out for a couple of hours. He knows where I'm going, what I'm going to do . . . down an unfamiliar street into an impersonal underground, I get into a train and ride . . . ride . . . ride . . . loosing time, seeing images of him and the girl . . . he touches her breasts, his long fingers feel the small, nipples through her summer dress. On the train taut nipples protrude through my light jumper. A man watches me, the train rocks, my husband pulls at the girl's tits; the man is nondescript, plain, inconsequential . . . flecks of dandruff show through his thinning hair . . . my husband squeezes the girl's breasts, pulling, hurting my tight nipples. The man on the train sits opposite me . . . he has dull eyes . . . my husband kneels in front of the red couch where the girl is sitting, slowly unzips her dress, he puts his mouth over her bare breasts and sucks, sucks, sucks. I feel his lips, she moans, his wet tongue teasing, in our dark bedroom I hear her sighs, her excitement excites me, my spirit transported, my big tits belong to someone else, my twitching body is her body . . . the train rocks , the man gestures to follow him. We stop at a cheap hotel; in the room I undress, lie down, my legs spared wide . . . wide . . . right out. For a moment she resists then thrusts her cunt forward, into his face. He licks her like a thirsty animal, through her panties, sucks her juices, she moans, the sound that comes from my throat is not related to me, I'm wet through her wetness . . . his tongue is working, lips sucking through the silk panties he makes me wear, my husband's head is buried in between her legs, sighs fill the room , his fingers thrust up her ass, in the bare hotel room the man reams me, pumping, pumping, pumping in, in, in. The girl groans as the finger disturbs her shit, the man puts his penis inside my mouth, fucking my mouth he comes loudly, over my face, hair, throat. My husband on top of the girl is wild, squeezing hurting, pressing; the man ejaculates in my backside, the girl wants the finger higher, higher, higher; violently she comes . . . my face wet from my husband's spunk."

INGRID

In November of 1970 I went to Amsterdam for the first Wet Dream Festival – a sort of Cannes of porn – organized by Bill Levy and Jim Haynes, editors of Suck, the first European sex-magazine.

Ingrid, an erotic model from Copenhagen, was the star of the sex manifest.

She's a trendy, gay, kind, eighteen-year-old with lonely grey eyes. Rigidly macrobiotic, she preaches the virtues of brown rice. Artistic: she draws, embroiders, and sews her own clothes that oscillate from micro-shorts to long Indian velvets accompanied by feathery boas of deep colours that grace her slender white neck. She talks politics, involves herself with the alternative media, associates her erotic manifestations and free- love philosophy with revolution.

I don't perceive her as a revolutionary; but see her more as a victim of the new philosophy which has evolved from a new paradigm which decrees unfaithfulness a positive action, and has coined a new theory for promiscuity, terming it love and understanding of our fellow human beings (read: men). A credo that has its followers believe that jealousy and monogamy are petty and banal.

She's been drawn into the game of 'freedom' (read: no commitment); duped by the Hugh Heffners of the anti-establishment – men in flower-power guise: preachers of universal love – unable to love. These 'underground Casanovas' falsely set themselves up as sexual gurus, sexual potentates, humanitarians, wise men, sexual-gold-medallists flashing out fantasy images of themselves. Love-gods, who will soon get rid of you if you don't follow them, if you are not 'liberated'; which in their terms means you are not sitting with your mouth wide open in awe of the prick which will soon be coming into your it.

Nearly all the 'sex-impresarios' I've met, who are involved in propagating erotic scenes, orgies, so called pornographic movies and literature; who encourage women to fuck everybody – whether they do it under the guise of universal love, politics, life style, or whatever, have all been men passed their prime, who need props because they fear, and know, they are not capable of satisfying. In an orgy you can get a lot of mileage on a limp cock.

****

"Sometime I'm afraid that a man would think he could fuck very easily with me because I do porno films, but that's very old fashioned to think like that. I have real consciousness. Some really straight men, like some photographers, think, if she's done this then she's doing other things too, and then they're very rude when I don't do it. But all the nice men I know, I don't have any problem with them.

"I get forty pounds a day, you know – that's one day's exploitation. When you are a secretary you get forty pounds for two weeks. I think it's much more exploitation for a girl to sit there and always be the boss's girl, and always do what the boss says, than to do one day's nude modelling. Nobody can do you anything, nobody can tell you what you have to do, you can be yourself, you know. He can tell you smile, smile, but he still can't be really uptight on you, you know. But there are too many bad jobs around now. I don't want to do bad jobs, like bad porno films, where girls are fucked, but in really bad ways for the girls: really sadistic ways. Then I refuse.

"I don't fuck too much. I have trouble coming, you know. Even with my friend, you know. I don't know . . . when I think about it I can't think that I don't trust him . . . I really trust him, but still most times I don't come, you know. I come every time he licks my cunt, then I come every time, because he's very loving, he can do it very good. I don't know anybody who is doing it so nice as he. But really fucking fucking, I hardly ever come. And I think it's much nicer to come inside, it's much more whole; and it's much more involving. It's much higher. But it's very hard for me, very hard. I don't know why.

"Maybe it's because of the age, I don't know, I'm not sure. It depends when you start and how long you have been doing it for. Every month I'm enjoying it more, because I learn what is really nice and what is really best for me. Sometimes when you're very young you don't have the experience to know how good it can be and what you can reach. I think you even get hornier when you get older. Because I think I could be very, very horny, I think it is in me, but I'm not sure enough to really do it.

"Sometimes I am quite depressed over this, you know, because I really don't know why. And when I'm with somebody else, like this cat last night, who is really a lovely guy, you know; you should fuck with him sometime: he's very nice and loving and very soft. He's twenty four and very clean. Ugh, I hate men which look dirty; I could never fuck with someone like this. I'm scared of venereal disease . . . of a dirty prick which doesn't smell good . . .

"And you know, sickness is something I really hate, because I was never sick in my life, you know. And also, you know, because I'm macrobiotic I think it's very bad to mix your juices with people who are not macrobiotic, you know, because they're much more poisonous, because your bodily discharges come from what you eat.

"I dream about sex, and when you dream about something, I think that's the truest fantasy. If you can remember it afterwards there's really a very deep fantasy you have somewhere. A very deep wish of what you would like to have.

"I dream up situations with my boyfriend. When I was first with him I was very masochistic; I was always thinking . . . you know I was very young . . . seventeen. And I had a very bad experience with a man, you know, because the man who took away my virginity was very bad. It wasn't very nice for me, I didn't feel anything, you know, except the brutality. And that's why I always want brutality . . .

"It's only that women have always been under the men, you know, have always been suppressed, you know, and always been dominated by men, that they think it must also be in bed like that.

"Your mother tells you this. My mother always told me, don't trust men, they only want one thing. But I don't think that's always true.

"When I was first together with my boyfriend – it was too nice with him – you know, he was very loving, very soft, so I always make up fantasies like he would rape me or he would put me on the bed and fuck me from behind . . . be brutal, you know . . . being put on the bed and my legs spread out and really being held down tight and very badly, very roughly . . . but I don't think that's good. I think these fantasies of being dominated, being brutalized, degraded, you know, are not healthy. Now I'm at a stage, you know, when I speak to him very often about sex. He is very trusting and he always screams very much when he comes. You know, most men don't do that. Sometimes they moan a little bit, but not really loud, really hard. I like to scream myself; I think it's much better, much nicer when you really let yourself go.

"I like the yoga position where the man has his feet crossed and you sit on his prick and you have your legs around his back. You only rock a little bit gently and it's really quiet, you really concentrate on each other. And I like very much when I explore the man's body. I like to suck his prick, but I don't like them to come in my mouth; I like it when he comes inside me, you know. And I like to play around with it till it's really stiff, you know.

"Most people fuck for five minutes. It's long, five minutes, even. Sometimes we fuck for half an hour, forty-five minutes, but mostly when you're really horny fifteen minutes is really a long time.

"Sometimes I simulate, because I can't fuck anymore, you know. And I know that I can't come, so I simulate because he likes to come with me.

"We're already two years together, and always when I begin to play with him, immediately he has a very big erection, you know. I never came to him and took his prick in my mouth and it stayed limp. Immediately it grows.

"He's very much aware of his body, he's very exhibitionistic. Same with me, I know that I have a very nice cunt and I like to show it off.

"I really like to jump around and move. I'm not at all shy. I like to hold the prick; I like to put it in. I like to hold the eggs when we are fucking.

"Most girls are not like this, I know because my boyfriend always tells me I'm the nicest fuck he has, you know; because all the time he fucks with other girls he says it's not so nice because they can't rhyme so much, they can't make such nice movements, you know. I can't come, but I love movements.

"I have fantasies of a very sexually liberated life. That the men who live with me, they understand me, you know. When they would come into a room and I would be fucking with somebody they would go out again; or if they like the other person they would come to us.

"If it would be a girlfriend of mine I would also want to have a very nice relationship with her. I would like to fuck with her, you know, to be very gentle with her; and I would like to hold and caress her, and I wouldn't mind if she would be the third person.

"We are already two years together and he's fucked with other girls only since three months. All the other time he was only fucking with me.

"Sometimes when I was away he was fucking with other girls, but very rarely; like once every two months or so. Now he's fucking very often, like once a week or twice a week, with some other girls. But he thinks it's good for him because he's very curious, you know. He wants to have a good scene with everybody. And he's so lovely, he's so nice, many girls want to fuck him. Many girls they really run after him like mad, you know, and he can't resist them.

"Before he didn't like to communicate with many people, only with me, but now it's different. And it's better for him to communicate with many people. And he thinks if you really want to communicate with somebody very good you have to fuck with them too; and he thinks it's very important.

"He tells me every time it's not so nice and whole and so harmonic like it is with me, you know; but it's something else; you know.

"He's twenty-six, he likes independence, and it's good because I have more money than he has and I feel very independent because it's mostly my money we spend. But he thinks I'm too dependent on him, and that's why he said I should go away; I should see what it's like to be alone, because I was never alone. But now I can be. It was only fear of me – insecurity – so I made it easy for myself, and was never alone. But now I can, and he was right; he knew I would be feeling much better if I went away for a while. I was very thankful to him that he did that. Alone I wouldn't have done it. And he explained everything, because he loves me very much and he wants that I'm happy too, and he thinks that you only can be happy when you have such a free relationship with other people, and I think it's true.

"Sometimes I have fantasies of big tits, you know. Sometimes I really think how it would be to fuck with big tits. I really get horny when I think of my boyfriend fucking with a girl with big tits, you know. I have very small ones, but I don't like to have big ones because it's too much; it's always in your way, it wobbles and it doesn't look so nice, it sages down easy.

"Sometimes I masturbate and think . . . When he's away and I know he's not coming home, and I know that he's fucking with somebody else and I don't know who it is, then sometimes I think, you know, that he would be fucking with a girl with big tits. And I could imagine that he would be more brutal to a woman with big tits; she's always more womanly, motherly. And if a girl has big tits you really feel it in a totally different way and aggression against all that softness takes place, and you really want to do something bad to it.

"I know when he's with a special chick which I don't like. She's very tiny and very thin, but she has very big tits . . . they are really big . . . look like they have milk inside. And he's rubbing his prick on them, and he has a very big erection – his prick is sooo big – and I think that he's rubbing his prick on her all over. Between the tits and on the tits, pressing it into her nipples, then over her whole body.

"And he's putting his hand on her arse . . . and his prick inside her arse and he's rocking her, and she's not doing very much. She's very, very passive; and he's fucking her from behind, and he's very brutal; very hard. And then he licks her cunt and she's wrapping her breasts around his big erection. They lie together and he's rubbing his prick on her back . . . very sensual.

"Then he goes down on her cunt and she licks his prick, sucking it hard; and he pulls her hair, buries her head inside his legs and goes into her biting her tits; and he goes into her hard and goes faster and faster. They really hit it and he's kneading her tits and then he comes . . . he screams . . .

"But I don't think of these things when he's fucking with me. Sometimes I think of it the day or the night before I go to sleep, but I don't think of these things when he's fucking me.

"But sometimes when he's away, when I know he's fucking with somebody else, you know, when I know that he's gone away and he's not coming home – I don't know who it is you know, I could imagine him with a girl with big tits – but I think it would be much nicer if he wants to fuck with somebody that he would bring this girl home, you know. I could be with them too, you know; it's not nice to be alone . . . "

IRIS

Spaced out by Spring I doodle poems on the train, wishing I could go on travelling through the pastel landscape and following the margarine sun. An hour later, I'm nervous at approaching the unknown woman – friend of a friend – on her sexual fantasies.

We meet at her two storied white plastered suburban house. Five small rooms cluttered with indistinct, conventional furniture, pale green wall-to-wall carpets, a lovely marble table in the dining room, framed prints on ivory tinted walls, chintz windows curtained. The kitchen is fully equipped: dishwasher, Kenwood mixer, a large freezer where the food is neatly wrapped in plastic wrappers. A cleaner comes in three times a week to do the heavy house-work.

Iris Farmer is fifty-two years old. Shoeless, robed in a Westernized kaftan (the tent to contain her self-conscious overweight), she greets me warmly. Her thick pan-cake makeup accentuates the deep furrows on her animated face. There's a theatrical air – brisk, gay movements – about her. A full mouth rimmed with bright-red lipstick, she talks in upper class accent. Her short, softly premed blond hair is coloured blonde.

She's nervous, clearly she has been drinking, and tells me she suffers suicidal symptoms due to amphetamine withdrawal. After seventeen years on slimming pills, her habit was recently abruptly cut off without substitute by her doctor, when the addictive chemical capsule which gave her speedy energy, kept her from boredom and from getting fatter, was put on the dangerous list by the government.

Her hirsute son brings us milky coffee in the carefully landscaped garden, then continues building the fishpond. He lives in a bed sitter in Islington; she affectionately tells me; has a close relationship with her and visits often.

She's been married for twenty-nine years. Her husband is a company director. They have an income of thirteen-thousand a year, drive a Bentley, vote conservative, favour historical dramas and news programs on their black and white. He reads The Times; *she belongs to the local library.*

They go to church on Sundays, theatre is her favourite treat and once a week she plays bridge, but no longer frequents the "dull, gossipy suburban coffee mornings". For the last seven years they have slept in separate bedrooms.

Born to middleclass Victorian parents, who, she tells me, restricted her intellectually for fear she might learn some unsavoury facts, Iris was a virgin when she got married, but some years ago has had irregular, inconsequential affairs.

I left her feeling sad and angry, this woman I see as a misplaced person, a casualty of hypocrisy whose life's potential is wasted in alienation.

****

"I love my husband, in the sense that I've been with him a very long time. Like you love a dog you've been with a long, long time. It's companionable, and it gets better as you get older – the urge to break away is no longer strong . . .

"I've never realized my fantasies. This business of a threesome or a foursome; I don't think I would do it really.

"I think there are dreams essential to women as they grow older, to take your mind off your husband a little bit. Because he doesn't bring anything new to you, you have to create it, don't you?

"Everyone in the suburbs has affairs, but of course they're very discreet. It's easy, you meet a man in town, you make an appointment to meet him – say at a motel . . .

"I remember going along a very quiet road and there was a gypsy on a cart, and he bawled out the most obscene things to me and I thought it was wonderful. I loved it, you see, but I wouldn't stop. Because he might smell, you see, and if I could smell him, I would die.

"Sexually I've always been very . . . well . . . I could reach a climax in the middle of the road. And I could have many in the course of making love. And I could keep it up for ages, but of course my husband can't . . .

"Now sex bores me because I find he's lacking in imagination. He doesn't sort of prepare me, as it were, you know. He just suddenly says, well I think I'll do it, and that repulses me. I'd rather masturbate . . .

"I masturbate all the time, with anything that's available – the handle of the Hoover, candles, doorknobs. The *Pifco's* too quick, but I would imagine a nice machine . . .

"It's very curious really, because I used to be such a romantic person. I wanted love and moonlight and all the sort of things that go with it . . .

"I tried to discuss my fantasies with my husband, but he just grins at me. I ask him if he has any and he says he doesn't think so.

"There's something wrong with bloody men, isn't there? You see, when you consider it, you get all those books on how to look nice for your husband, how to behave for your husband. Why the hell don't they write books how husbands should look for their wives? The whole thing is male dominated. It makes me sick. All the time we must do our hair this way, and we must wear this, for a man who doesn't even care who you are . . .

"In marriage you stop seeing each other. I think women need a lot of little extra things. You see, if men only occasionally thought of a little extra something to bring home to their wives. It doesn't have to be a car. A little something to match their eyes.

"My age women are really fed up. I think secretly we wish we could be like our kids . . . get around . . . sleep around. Because with most of us it was correct to get married, and we did.

"I think personally life with a woman would be a marvellous life. You have understanding. My own fantasies have been lesbian for a long time. I didn't know about lesbianism when I was young. In my days things weren't discussed that much and right up until I was about thirty I never even knew what a lesbian was or heard about it. So I wonder perhaps if I were eighteen again and knew what I know today that I might be a lesbian. I don't know. It fascinated me. But on the other hand I was in London two or three years ago and a woman came up, started chatting, you see and suddenly I realized that she was a lesbian, you see. She asked me where I was going and I said I was going back to F., so she said, would you like to come back to my flat and have lunch? And it was what I've always dreamed of doing and I panicked . . . I dared not go. And this again, in my case, is because I have got very fat and ugly and I feel that would upset me. Had I been beautiful . . . I know that I haven't anything to offer bodily. But I don't think it's altogether that. I think I panicked. Then again I went to a party a while ago and I saw a lesbian there. You see I keep meeting them now because I know about them. They may know that I know. But as soon as they touch me I have no desire for them at all. I would rather it remained a fantasy. I don't really want to be a lesbian, inside myself. I know this for certain. It's just an idea and it's exciting, so therefore when I make love to my husband I'm thinking about all these erotics, you see – lovely things that lesbians would do, so that I enjoy my husband more, you see.

"With a woman I'd be the aggressive one. Oh yes, I imagine it all, I imagine the instruments we could use, the things we could do to each other. Women would know all the erotic parts. You're bound to know how to touch another woman, you can't help yourself. You know the parts, the pressure to apply. And I would like to wear an instrument.

"I would like to strap one on me and be on top of a woman, penetrating her and at the same time caressing her soft body. And be as filthy to each other as we like. Oh yes, I imagine it all; but you've got to be young to have done it. I'm too old. Because I would hate an old woman, but then I'd hate a young one because I feel I wouldn't be nice enough for her . . .

"The women around here don't talk much. They wouldn't tell me they masturbate, for instance. That's a word they don't say. The sort of women that live around here would like you to think that when they had a baby it was by Immaculate Conception. I know one woman, she told me she had her son and then from then on she never looked at her husband again. I wanted to know what she did, but she didn't want to talk about it – changed the subject. I couldn't push on; you couldn't push on with these kinds of women in the suburbs. They're afraid of their secrets, you see; they're all appearing to be someone. I don't know how much they are or how much background they've got, one doesn't really know . . . I suspect very little, some of them. They're new rich, as it were.

"They never let their hair down, you never know any of them really . . . it's quite curious. And everyone always pulling everybody to pieces, you can feel the nastiness . . . bitchiness.

"They've got to have their cars, their china, someone to do the housework; but they don't give the kids the right food. The appearance is so important; for me too, I'll do the right things, I don't want to be considered peculiar. You get lost eventually. I've had it. Your emotions get . . . you just change, and you don't change because you want to change – people change you. Their values are all wrong, there's no warmth. They don't want to know. You can stay here and rot and die . . . . quite easily . . . nobody cares . . .

"We're the pillars of the church and we're very respectable, but whether we have secrets deep down, we never tell. It's such a lonely existence. Of course I've got the dog and the garden; they mean a lot to me. Funny, at one time I used to think I was quite an interesting person. I think I was, at one stage . . . when I was young. It's not like that now. Living in suburbia is a killer because you can't be yourself, you see. In the end you don't know who you are, so you get confused and the point is, you don't bother. You don't care what you are. You just go on living really.

"I've got a couple of hundred sleeping pills, which one day, if it gets too bad I'll take . . .

"It's a beautiful life, a gift, and it shouldn't be like this, should it . . . ?"

JUDITH MALINA

Judith Malina is a great actress, writer, poet and director, who with her husband, Julian Beck, founded The Living Theatre.

We were both living in Rome in the seventies, and became friends.

She told me she had read my book when it was first published, and was always sorry that she hadn't known me at the time as she would have loved to give me her thoughts on women's sexuality and their sexual fantasies.

And so I interviewed her in May of 1979

****

HK: Judith, why do you think sex has such a turbulent fascination for us?

JM: Because we experience a dualism in our sexual lives. We understand that there is a librating key through our bodies and their union with other bodies. Yet each of us knows how sex becomes an obstacle because we are bound to a heavy sexual mythology. This mythology confuses the quest for truth with sexual adventure, or an obstacle to sexual truth: as in the pursuit of the Holy Grail. And it is a present in all our literature. Faust, who wants to reach God, reaches only the demonic forces and the spirit that negates, for and through the beauty of Helen of Troy.

We are all Faust searching for something we know to be related to our physical, sexual and sensual reality. And we find ourselves in Faust's hell, or in Dante's saying: 'But look at Paolo and Francesca, burning in hell forever in the Divine Comedy – an image of the total bliss of being together – even in hell, forever.' And you as a woman and I as a woman have experienced this search and this profound disappointment. But we also have the moments of hope, when we see a human relationship the way it should be all the time.

In the love relationship we find ecstasy which should be ours because we have it in us to experience it. And if and when it shatters and seems like an illusion, our hearts are broken.

But it was not an illusion. It was the truth that shows us what is possible between human beings. Sex is an obstacle and a hope; we move between these two polarities and most of us fall into an abyss between them. The object of feminist sexuality is to break this pattern.

I can't adjust my body to living without a man very easily, though I see a certain virtue in being able to do it. I think no relationship is better than a makeshift, unsatisfying, trivial relationship. But I feel the cycles of change in my body very strongly. I feel changes in temperature, weather and diet, in an almost exaggerated way. In the same way, if I deprive my body of sex, or limit my masturbation, it interferes with my capacity to work, and that's what I want to be able to do well.

When I don't have a lover I tend to break down, I feel weak and frightened, I tend to get hysterical symptoms, everything troubles me, small things drive me up the wall, I shout angrily at my family, I'm hypersensitive at rehearsals, I go through depression. I feel my own bio–rhythmic changes very specifically.

When I don't have a satisfying sexual relationship I find I think about sex all the time, the way when you haven't enough to eat you think of food all the time, the way when you're really strung for money you think about money all the time, because there is a balance in life and conditions are in disequilibrium when they become critical. And that diminishes the energy function. We only have a certain amount of strength, energy, and power. Our bodies generate a capacity for so much, and if we take it away in one area we drain ourselves. Whereas in a deeper relationship over a period of time, the sexuality gives energy, strengthens the mind and body, spirit and soul.

I experienced a period of celibacy in my life once, and if I had to face it again I know I would face it more bravely. At the time I was forty–three or forty–four, and I had terrible fears that I had lost the secure ground I had stood on for so long – my sexual attractiveness, my sexual experience with men and women. I was afraid, I became desperate.

Many times during the period in which I was in this dilemma I asked myself how can it be no one wants me? I'm still a very attractive creature, with much to give, open to love . . . I went to people who had loved me for years and said, 'Now I'm seeking love,' and they looked at me and said 'No'. And I thought: 'My God, it's because I'm forty–four years old! But it wasn't, it was because they felt from me a cry to which they had to say no. Not until I met Hanon, who, as you know, is much younger than me, and entered into a very happy love relationship could I see what had happened. The pressure, the desperation are an obstacle to sexual relationship. This fear seems to keep possible lovers at a distance; if we encounter them, we repel them in a way that they themselves don't understand. It's very mysterious, but it can be overcome.

HK: Many men prefer younger women.

JM: Yes. The positive side of the love of men for younger women is a love of the purity and innocence, the trufulness, the openness and potential of those women who don't bear the burdens of maturity. On the other hand much of it can be an avoidance of what a relationship with a mature woman means to a man. One way in which men avoid women being real for them is to relate only to young women who haven't yet asserted themselves and on whom they try to imprint their authority. They excuse their behaviour by saying: 'She's only a girl, she'll get over it. This is part of her education.' To be seduced and betrayed, that is, again and again; until we become hard and tough and able to defend ourselves and then they don't want us because we're hard and though and able to defend ourselves.

Right now almost everybody I know feels lost. Men are frightened by what's happening to women, frightened and not sure whether they should be patiently open to feminism, or whether they should fight back. Many men retreat into the homosexual relationship which is much safer for a man today than the relationship with a woman, and somehow socially more approved.

But where does that leave us?

HK: Do you consider yourself lucky, Judith?

JM: I've certainly always been aware of my luck. First of all I've spent most of my adult life with Julian, and to share with one other person all your hopes and visions and work, is a very great privilege. Having that, how can you not think you're lucky?

This is a very joyous time for me because of Hanon who sees our delicate, imbalanced relationship, the love of two people of different generations, from such a profound prospective that he makes possible the seemingly impossible. We both had to allow ourselves to become perilously vulnerable, and this vulnerability is related to pacifism.

That's what Gandhi was concerned about. He was concerned about opening yourself up to the person you confront: but not to their enmity, rather to their empathy and potential warmth.

Historically this is reflected in the sexual situation in which women now find themselves confronted by the one who is certainly not the enemy, but the lover, and yet the one who offers us the greatest opposition to our lives.

Hanon and I used to have terrible, terrible fights, as I suppose most lovers do. They were bitter and they were brutal, violent and hard. But now after almost a year we found that we've been able to observe our behaviour and we began to see, after a while, in the context of our intimacy, how this pattern developed and we found that there is a certain point on the downhill at which you can't save anything, you can only hope it doesn't become violent, hope it doesn't become fatal to that relationship. This happens at a moment in which a psychic change takes place. There's a flickering moment, which you begin to watch, you can feel in your body when you click into anger. It feels as if some physical current were changed, as if the voltage were changed, as if the metabolism were suddenly quickly reorganized. On one level you might say that at that point the negative aspects are in control.

But there's an earlier moment to which we can become sensitive when there's a possibility with a lot of love to turn it on the Gandhian principle of Ahimsa. It's important personally, sexually, even politically to recognize that moment and then turn it. The Gandhian turn means to look at the other person and say: 'What does he want? What does he need?' instead of 'What do I need?' And at that moment the rest of the seemingly inevitable downwards skid doesn't have to happen.

Hanon and I patiently examine how we reach this point. I ask myself at what point did I say something hurtful; he asks himself at what point did he say something hurtful to me. So we go back and trace the minute and terribly boring details of action. But the development of feeling is not boring at all, but fascinating to examine. To look at how our feelings in the last five minutes changed from a certain point, then bang, suddenly we're at rock bottom, and we're at the real problem which has nothing to do with who slammed the door, but which has to do with the deepest contradictions and suffering of our life.

HK: How do you and Julian and Hanon work together?

JM: I'm a political person, I want to contribute to finding ways we can live together in peace. I am dedicated to that, and so are Hanon and Julian.

For a long time we three were lovers together and after a while Hanon and I moved into a deeper sexual relationship, while the creative aspect between the three of us deepened into work relationship, in which we've created major plays together.

The depth of the dimension between three people who have had the kind of history and the kind of sensibility that the three of us have is very extraordinary for us. We treat each other as an extremely creative event.

HK: Do you suffer sexual jealousy, Judith?

JM: Oh yes. I've never really told the truth about what I think about jealousy, because I've always been intimidated by the socially accepted premise, that jealousy is a weakness of character, a crime of possessiveness and authoritarianism, a sin contrary to the basic tenets of human individual liberty.

I read an article the other day by a woman who said the problems she'd encountered in her own sexual liberation is the replacement of the commandment: 'Thou shall not commit adultery' with 'Thou shall not be jealous,' and that the one as well as the other causes the restrictions inherent in commandments.

Yes, it is an affliction, but we don't want to think of it as a sin or a crime, no, jealousy isn't a sin, nor is it a crime – it's *the* tragedy of human life. The fact that love is not immortal is a fact that no one wants to face. We feel if anything is eternal this feeling must be what eternity is about, because that's what we feel when we love. That's the knowledge that we have at the moment of love and so we must connect it with eternity and with endurance. We say I love now and forever, and at the moment when forever seems to end our hearts break.

There's an old rhyme that says 'Hegamous, higamous men are polygamous; higamous, hegamous women are monogamous.' And what is really so curious and what we seem to be historically overlooking, because we believe in equality, and the political ideal that we should be equal, is the biological difference

God knows women have been oppressed, repressed, harnessed, raped, wounded, exploited, and so it follows that we demand equality. But the biological difference expresses itself in evolutionary terms: the fact is that biologically a woman is capable of having 20 children at maximum. Given the circumstances of life most women not only don't have that many but are incapable of that, and certainly they don't want to. Men, on the other hand, are biologically, if not circumstantially, capable of having thousands of children. We don't like to face this; we don't like to see this as one of our realities – that's a sexist notion.

Now it seems probable that it was both the error and the wisdom of women that created marriage; as much as the tendency of the man to bind to him the woman – we haven't talked about men's jealousy – because men's jealousy doesn't express itself in suffering so often as it expresses itself in prohibitative laws and in repressive measures and violence. Just when we become masochiststic, they become sadistic.

But when we speak as feminists today of the necessity of feminizing our whole civilization, or feminizing the culture and of the need of men to become more feminized, the men are offended, defensively they believe we want them to behave like transvestites: dressed in feminine clothing. They know what we are really asking; we're asking them to be softer and more responsible.

Jealousy is never good because no kind of anger is ever good. No one can justify any feeling less than love. Where there is total trust there is no jealousy. Now, trust for what? I'm not sure because that relates to something which is a philosophical stumbling block called the meaning of truth. In daily life it works itself out on a practical level. For instance, trust that everything that you say is the best you know – whenever you open your mouth it's the truth coming out of your mouth. You may not always know what the truth is, but if you know, you are going to tell it. The idea of any kind of deception between us should become unthinkable. The way I wouldn't hit you I wouldn't lie to you.

I may, sometime, in a moment of rage feel such an impulse, but I wouldn't do it. I may in some moment of confusion or embarrassment desire to lie, but I shouldn't do it. We feel certain disgust with the morality of Sunday school because in our experience it has gone hand in hand with the greatest hypocrisy – just as many who have preached pure love have set up hurtful murderous structures. The hypocrisy of organized religion has despoiled the concepts of what is really necessary. The gap between the word love as a religious experience, and love as a sexual experience, and love as a domestic experience has been shattered into smithereens. We can't pull ourselves together.

Two people confront each other across a barrier; but this barrier between any two people is not great compared to the vastness of the souls that are behind that barrier. So when we break through it's a real glimpse of what life could be like. It could be like that.

People are searching for something which is a higher form of communication between us. And this will become possible for us when we no longer have to fear each other.

We can't afford to reach that step which we sometimes call extra-sensory, in which we can touch each other on a deeper and higher level because the barrier of hostility makes knowledge far too dangerous. If I could enter your mind as I would like to enter your mind and then I have a hostile thought, I could kill you or harm you with that thought. So I can't enter your mind as long as such a possibility exists. But when that hurtful possibility no longer exists I think we will make breakthroughs that we can't even dream about today, because they sound like absurdities in the face of what's possible for us; given, alas, who we are and what we are.

The higamous hegamous, the polygamousness of the men and the monogamousness of women are the emblematic, the crucial point that the playwright chooses to show some profound human truth by showing two people confronting each other.

In order to show a reality of the profoundest scope, the artist puts two persons opposite each other and shows what conflict is and how it works itself out. In human life, when two people confront each other, this conflict of need and this polarity is for us, in the love relationship, always the emblem of the universe. But we've translated it into a kind of competitive sexual drive in order to accommodate our post–industrial vision of the world; so we see this duo-drama reflected that way.

Between every man and every woman this drama is enacted again and again; we are handing him the apple of truth and liberty and he is accusing us of being in pact with the devil.

HK: The photograph on the jacket of your book, *The Enormous Despair*, pictures you behind prison bars. How do you feel about bondage?

JM: The roots of sexual bondage are political as the roots of political bondage are sexual. Bondage expresses that in which one person yields all and the other person yields nothing. I've had some personal sexual experience in which bondage has played a part, though not the main part; but rather a part of a theatricalization of a master-slave relationship acted out in two people performing a sexual play.

I've had the experience and I wasn't really moved by the bondage, though I was interested in it because my lover was interested in the bondage. I was more moved by my fear of the blood and the knife. The bondage seemed to me relative to the political situation, and as we might talk for instance about the political situation between a man and a wife in a conventional marriage: the political relationship about who is boss and makes the decisions –who organizes what, who has the power of veto and so on.

When I was desperate for love I was able to engage in a sado-masochistic relationship because I couldn't feel anything and pain seemed like something still possible to feel. As Artaud says about the meaning of cruelty in the theatre – when all other possibilities are exhausted and there is nothing more we can feel, we can still feel physical pain. This is a negative experience in a negative field.

I was in such a case when I was enamoured with a man who played with me this strange and dangerous game. And that's what's the matter with it – that someone can get hurt, and the violence implicit in that is untenable. Can't do anything in the name of love that hurts someone. But the ecstasy of breaking out of the taboo is a very dramatic ecstasy. In the bondage metaphor the political relationship becomes clear. It becomes clear that we're again acting out the police and the people being policed.

HK: Tell me about your 'Knife and Blood' experience.

JM: Knife and blood came into my life at a time when I was very depressed; in a situation when I had no lover and was unable to cope with the empty space. And into this space came a man with a heavy prototypical masculine fantasy. A sadistic fantasy.

O. was a very good actor/performer and consequently able to translate into a sexual relationship a high theatricality and a ritualistic quality which appealed to my sense of drama and also to my desperation.

This man, an Argentinean of Spanish parentage, saw himself as a cultural and mythic descendent of a certain image of a Spaniard. Of an Iberian image, of the power, 'The Man': his readiness with the knife to defend himself, his attributes, his possessions, his honour.

And this man seduced me at a time when I was vulnerable and promised to show me the most extreme and extravagant sensual experience. Promised to teach me an ecstasy beyond any I had ever felt, if I were willing to take the consequence of enacting a totally submissive masochistic role. He said at the beginning that this might lead to my death, but that it would do so at a point at which I were willing to let that happen.

I was frightened but I hoped that my life instincts would protect me. They almost didn't. In fact I was finally saved by another woman.

O. took me on a slow trip that began with glimpses of the sensations that relate to pleasure in the body. An analysis of them, an understanding of them. A definition between the fine line between pain and pleasure to develop in me a capacity to increase pleasure as I increase pain.

He did this by slow stages beginning with the experiences of the pain/pleasure syndrome that everyone experiences in normal sexual life. As one might easily enjoy some times being lovingly bitten, or feel the whirl of fingernails.

O. began with these and developed in the parts of my body which were most sensitive to such experiences: the acceleration of the pleasure and acceleration of the pain in parallel; leading to a situation in which I was constantly anxious for more pain in order to experience more pleasure to a point of incredible ecstasy.

This happened in Brazil, in a small hotel off Ipanema beach: a very romantic setting; at a time when we were creating the *Legacy of Cain*: the play about political sado-masochism. And what interested me was the discovery of the principle which allowed the masochist to bear the pain as translatable into our political reality in which the mass of the people allow themselves to be oppressed and suffer all the time, while a small ruling class is somehow, in our social structure, in a position in which they get all the benefits.

To understand the pattern that makes sexual submission possible, and prevents revolution in the sense that you and I would like to see revolution – which is not a bloodbath in the streets – I was interested in how I acted it out with O.

The same submission that works itself out sexually is a pattern for our social life and we have to see it, we have to shed light on it. To see how we act that out. I was interested in the scenario he created for my role as the submissive, because certainly in any Sadomasochistic drama I would never play the sadist. Does it then follow that I have to play the masochist? Camus said "Let's be neither victims nor executioners," and I agree, we should not be victims, though never at the cost of being executioners.

And in our bedroom both O. and I, who were both aware of this because we were working on the play together, enacted this cruel and inhuman relationship, and it betrayed in me something I never otherwise felt: which is a suicidal tendency.

I'm not a suicidal person; sometimes I despair, but I could never imagine . . . And yet on some certain level O. and I were in conspiracy together against my body.

None of this could have happened without my consent. Nothing was happening that I was not agreeing to. I just had to go away, or walk out of the room, nothing was holding me; but emotionally I became quite incapable of walking away.

I would have been dead within a few months given the acceleration at which our drama was going: the physical components of what actually happened were very frightening. The actual enactments of the knife and blood.

I said once to O."Why is this so exciting? Is it because it's against the morality?" And he said, "No, it's because it's against the ethic." And I thought that was a rather good insight, because the morality is a code but the ethic is the foundation on which we live together as human beings.

We were playing with human relationship, and whether or not what *he* was doing was unholy, what *I* was doing was unholy because it was against my body. Not to hurt anybody is anyone's basic commitment, and I could not justify it. I suffered terribly and I found myself trapped the way you are trapped in a free-fall where there is nowhere to go but down. I couldn't even see running away because the only bondage was in my mind.

And then there came my guardian angel — a beautiful and wonderful woman. An actress, the daughter of a famed Brazilian poet: a woman of intelligence and great spirit. And she fell in love with me and I fell in love with her, and O. fell in love with her and she fell in love with O. And she took him away and saved me.

HK: Tell me about your sexual fantasies

JM: My fantasy life is such a structured, careful life. It's such a delicate life — this is of course the problem of fantasy; it's woven of such a delicate web, that speaking about it in some way diminishes it. My fantasy experience takes on a pageant-like, epic form because I'm a theatrical person. It's a complex world picture; an immense fictional world into which I enter.

I've had all my life this benign cannibalistic fantasy with an extravagant scenario. Benign in the sense that while the fantasies were certainly gory in terms of real-world reality, they contained no malevolent experiences.

What takes place in these fantasies is an extreme lust and desire in which there was no aggressor. There may be an eater and an eaten, but neither the giver nor the taker is infringing upon the desire of the other, but rather expressing their own desire, which coincides with the desire of the other.

This is the groundwork of a kind of fantasy in which one could commit ultimate acts without suffering. In my fantasy nothing is ever taken, everything is ecstatically given. I don't want to be tied up; I want to spend the rest of my life in the ecstatic pleasure of becoming part of the body of those I love.

If I imagine myself in a fantasy to be splendidly devoured by the one I love, or many I love, nothing about it is negative. It's a total body union, which means that the termination of my life is a high point of ecstatic union in which there is nothing but sheer joy as long as I'm aware the pain all transformed into the most ecstatic pleasure: into a feeling of pleasure as intense as a great feeling of pain.

Now, as I have no need in real life to have to devour anybody or be devoured by anybody, I have no inclination to make my fantasies come true.

LAURA

At thirty-nine Laura looks older, with an undistinguished face whose prominent feature is her vivid blue eyes. She wears a grey skirt of no determined length; her brown hair is in page-boy style.

She runs a small pre-school play group, and lives in a tiny, neat apartment in Covent Garden, where rents are cheap. There are antimacassars on the compact armchairs; a Siamese cat naps on the tidy, dark velvet cover on the bed by the window. A patterned Wilton dominates the floor; two Tretchkoff prints decorate the off-white walls; a vase filled with multicoloured plastic flower sits on the mantelpiece of a non-functional fireplace. Photographs of children she has cared for stand framed on small tables among aspidistras and potted violets.

She takes yearly chartered holidays to somewhere in Europe. She doesn't smoke; sometimes has a small tumbler of sweet sherry. She tells me that she really loves children, always involving herself with them and their upbringing, and is against working mothers. She says a child needs the care of its mother and substitutes are never satisfactory. I feel attacked and argue that in cases like mine where the money I earn is our only income, it is absolutely necessary to be working. She agrees, but nevertheless leaves me with the feeling that she judges critically.

She's brisk, mannish in her gestures, offers me tea; she's a virgin, she says. I'm surprised that she agreed to talk to me.

****

"Of course I'd like a relationship with a man, but it seems I let it go too far now. I don't meet many men who are of my age and single – certainly not interesting men, or men who I would appeal to. Then I have a fear of men – I simply don't believe I would be able to have intercourse.

"My father was Irish; he married my mother here who was from London. I suppose we were upper-working class. He was a mechanic, earned quite good money, drank a lot, treated my mother very badly; but when he died of bronchitis, almost twenty years ago now, she missed him.

"I didn't want that kind of marriage. Of course I fantasized thatched cottages in remote areas; the fireside, the pipe and slippers, homemade jams; but I'm fully aware that that's a common fantasy and seldom and seldom realized successfully.

"Everyone has fantasies, of course. But I don't have sexual ones anymore now. A woman's body is geared to forget about sex if it is not available. I simply don't think about it. When I was much younger I had a recurring dream.

"I remember very vividly as it happened so many times. I even realize the significance of it. You see, I had a very strict Catholic upbringing. When I was in the convent the girls used to finger each other, always in the dormitory at night. But I always rejected that – I was frightened of the sin I would be committing.

"I realize now that sex is not a sin that it's a natural process, but it seems my parents had programmed me thoroughly. I t was one of my father's greatest fears that I should lose my virginity before marriage. Things were like that then, and as you see, I never found anyone to marry. I don't feel bitter about it, it certainly isn't something that nags my everyday life, but then as I said, at times I fantasize.

"Well I suppose you want to know about my dream. I shall tell you in detail . . .

"I'm in a convent. Physically it's not the same one, where I had been as a child, but it's the same one, only more abstract. I suppose like all dreams it has a surrealistic quality about it – everything here seems to be more feeling than visual – but I can see it in my mind very clearly.

"It's a very depraved convent where the girls are kept for the pleasure of the priests and especially the bishop, who is a very frightening figure in his gaudy cloak, tall hat and piercing eyes. There is so much scarlet around him, that I suppose he's really Satan.

"There is a mother superior who is a lesbian who reports you to the bishop if you do anything wrong.

"Then the bishop orders me into a corner, with my hands tied behind me; and first he fingers me, and then the mother superior, and then anyone who might come by is allowed to touch me. It's very twisted because I have to resist my physical pleasure as part of my religious duty.

"After the punishment sessions I have to go to confession to the priest. He is very vivid, the priest, very frightening in a little dark confessional, and he smells stuffy from his black cloth which he has worn for far too long. And he cross-questions me and finds that in fact I had enjoyed being touched and fingered, and he tells me that I've been very bad and that I'll have to do penance, but first of all he gives me absolution, which happens in the confessional you see, and he tells me to lean over and hold up my skirt. He does it to me with a candle, which is the holy candle; and then he says,

I think I better give you a practice in this particular bit that you enjoy, and he leads me into his bedroom which is next door to the confessional.

"It's a beautiful bedroom, very luxurious and has a four-poster bed; tapestries and paintings and gold candelabras, and he is once again the frightening bishop, and makes me lie down on the bed and does his fingering all over again. Then he takes his clothes off and he has an enormous membrane, which would rip me apart, but just before penetration I wake up. And I've been very frightened."

LOUISE

Louise was sent to Summerhill when she was two-years old. Founded by A. S. Neill, the school is a progressive, co-educational, residential school, noted for its philosophy that children learn best with freedom from coercion. All lessons were optional, and pupils free to choose what to do with their time. To this day she looks at Neal as her father figure, and only writes in upper-case letters.

She was sent away at such an early age because of certain second-world-war conditions, but basically, she says, because her mother, a Jewish intellectual, didn't want children around. And so she was brought up in this alternative commune, a substitute home she loved, but which in many ways was no more than a jazzed-up orphanage.

When she was fifteen she returned home. Some months later her mother died, so she left once again; trained as a secretary and wandered around the outskirts of London.

She first had sex when she was sixteen. The experience was traumatic. He was her girlfriend's lover, she felt guilty, bad; there was neither enjoyment nor warmth in the event.

At twenty-three she married and lived in the suburbs. The relationship was friendly but virtually sexless, most of the emotions directed into the child, a boy, Richard, who is now ten.

Then she met Mike, fell in love with him, left her husband, moved to London. They've been together for seven years and have a three-year old girl, Mary.

She says that until quite recently she felt guilty about fucking, quite likely because of the first bad experience, she adds.

She never dared to admit she liked it so much, that she was and still is ashamed of some of her fantasies, perhaps the fantasy about her son in particular.

Visually Louis's life is drab: a lat in an impersonal red-brick building in Hammersmith; a Victorian settlement: long grey corridors with doors leading into small square rooms where the children run free. Much of her time is spent in the kitchen where she cooks, irons, thinks. Meals round the wooden table usually include friends.

She cleans the house, on Thursdays she goes to the laundry, she cooks the meals, darns the socks, irons the shirts, washes the lavatory, gets up in the morning to make the breakfast. She hates it, she says, suffers from the hardship, resents the lack of time, the unwritten book which is in her head and which she hasn't the time to write. On the other hand she accepts the role in her particular relationship.

When Mike comes home she looks after him. He participates, but clearly his time consumption is alienated from that of his family. He's concerned with the intellect, with the acid culture, with his work as a teacher and with the play he is writing. He wants to make money – it would facilitate access to channels which could further his productivity.

They have to be frugal. The lights are off in rooms which are not in present use, the food is plain, they are careful with the telephone, and they don't go out much. When they do it's a hassle with the baby-sitters, always having to ask friend to do it, often having to pay emotional dues for the service. If they go to the West End and spend their money on a film which they don't enjoy, they resent it. But they are also mobile –they go into the country and visit friends, they get an overdraft and buy and old car that takes them around for a while until it breaks down. They take a tent and the children to Normandy and have a good time.

They quarrel, she threatens to leave, swears she would, but where could she go? Who would have her with two children and no money? He gets nasty: he's overworked and worried about finance. She gets fed up, she's exhausted and can't afford to buy a pair of shoes; her clothes are second-hand from jumble sales or hand-me-downs from friends.

Life is hard, beautiful, sad, and fun, she says. An invention – a creation of another world within this world. She can have any fantasy she wants, she says, because they are all available and she uses them for colour additives. She laughs a lot.

When she says that nothing counts for her except sex, the statement could be misinterpreted. She makes many things count. She loves people and life. At the launderette she gets involved with the one-legged fat lady who runs it and who traffics in pills on the side. Louise forms a conspiracy with her: she involves herself in the plot of scoring stuff she doesn't want which she then exchanges with others, enabling her to give, to please, and throw herself into further deals. A petty thief brings her goods which she sells for him; an unhappy woman goes to her for comfort. She's seldom alone. She takes an interest in the children's teachers, talks to the other mothers, smiles showing buck teeth, asks questions, gives advice, and handles herself with intelligence.

She smokes a lot of dope. As opposed to the suburban mind-deadening tranquilizer habit which seems to be the norm in London, she's into mind tripping exploration. She loves drugs, anything that will induce exciting chemical changes. She's modern: likes plastic; men going to the moon and the chemicals that are part of the age. She drops acid, and is capable of integrating the trip into her working day; and then brings herself down with Mandrax². Always there's hash, grass, and she's mind tripping all the time, but constantly remaining aware of herself and Mike and the children and people she loves.

When Louise takes a Mandrax in the evening, or plays her fantasy games with Mike she doesn't care about the reality. Because the reality is that Louise has taken a Mandrax in the evening and is performing a creative schizophrenic sex play with her man. She's into flesh and loves to get fucked and they do it all the time, they communicate with each other's bodies and that's how she releases tension. Sex to her is the basic underlying life-force stimulus and motivation drive.

****

"I've always had fantasies and I wake up every morning having sexual dreams . . . all my life, but I can't remember them because they're dreams. They're all chopped up, just quick flashes, not long drawn up stories. Mike says I masturbate in my sleep all the time.

"We're very open with each other, but I don't tell him everything . . . like he doesn't know half the fantasies that go in me. Like when I woke up this morning I was being fucked by thousands of people . . . the whole world. I just lie there getting and getting and getting it. I just lie there with my legs apart. I can fuck anyone, you see anyone of either sex. And when I was carrying Mary I masturbated all the time, four, five times a day and I wouldn't let Mike fuck me at all, all the time I was pregnant. I used to have all these fantasies and I used to masturbate in front of windows and things like that, you know, and I've only just told him about it . . . three years later. Eventually we tell each other everything.

"Mike and I both have a terrific thing about snakes. We really want to sacrifice a snake, but that's impossible, we can't do it, and so one of my fantasies is snakes. It's usually an orgy – an Eastern Bazaar type of thing . . . in a tent . . . very bright. Persian rugs and large cushions and thousands of people fucking, and men and boys and lots of snakes which fuck everybody – fuck two people at the same time – and bodies intermingling with beautiful emerald and ruby snakes. I can feel them all over me, everywhere possible, in every orifice, inside . . . in everything. In my mouth, up my arms, everywhere!

---

² The trade name of a barbiturate type sedative drug called methaqualone which was commonly prescribed as a sleeping pill by doctors in the 1960s

"We've always fucked a lot; we've always had that sort of relationship. That's all I think about – sex . . . that's the only thing that really means anything. And he's the only man that's been able to fuck me as much as I want it, that's probably the reason why I stayed with him.

"The games started about a year ago when Mike sort of said, we could be four people quite easily, you know; you can play it all . . . you can do it all . . . you can have it all . . . you can have it all with one person. One chick can be all the chicks. You can spend so much time and energy fancying chicks and going after them, making them, and anyway it's not very good, and two people can do it so much better because they know each other and all the embarrassment . . . all that's gone. And the more you do it the easier it becomes – that much more interesting . . .

"I suppose we've been through every possible way that two people could meet and have sex together. We've been through the whole courtship, still having sex as ourselves, as Mike and Louise, but also having a courtship separately, a relationship separate from ourselves, where he tries to court me as a single chick, and that could last for three or four weeks before he actually got her into bed. And then we have one-night stands, a totally different thing – one night and that's it; you never see them again. And then it doesn't happen for two or three weeks, and then he comes in the evening as somebody different. He knocks on the door, says he's come to see us, or to see somebody else and I say, they're not in but you can wait, and we play things out. But we're also Mike and Louise . . . putting children to bed . . . being their parents . . . entertaining friends; so it's always a dual thing, because there's children and they have to be looked after and there's a whole lot going on outside the fantasy.

"I can't remember all the things he's been, all the things I've been. When we went to Brighton we met at Victoria Station, two separate people, he was a film director and I was trying to get a part in his film – a starlet – so he wasn't treating me very well.

"I've been raped, obviously. We've been through all those variations and I've raped him. It's difficult, we don't have the same ones more than about three or four times, than it's finished – so it becomes difficult to remember. He's been a dirty old tramp that I've picked up. I love dirty old tramps, and we play that one. He's really dirty – filthy. He doesn't take a bath for about three days and he's really dirty and he stinks. I dig that. And sometimes he says he'll be a young boy that I would seduce . . . or an older woman. He likes that one. He likes being a chick who seduces me – he dresses up as a chick. People have given us weird clothes and . . . nylon nighties with lace frills for instance . . . Mike puts them on

"But when we start to fuck then the whole thing goes, the whole game is finished. I stop being that person and he stops being that person when we're close to an orgasm. I can't fantasize an orgasm, I can't make one come through fantasy, but it doesn't matter if I don't always have an orgasm; I like sex without always having to have an orgasm.

"I make up the fantasies usually. He usually just likes to follow what I make up: whatever I fancy he should be, he would be.

"I get frightened sometimes. Sometimes you can be lost in the whole thing and when it gets too heavy I come back with a hell of a jerk calling his name out loud . . . to bring things back. It would be really quite easy for both of us to get lost in the fantasy. We're both schizophrenic . . . that's why we started. We really are four people – maybe because we are both Gemini and that's a double sign.

"I don't really know what real life is, but I think most of it is a fantasy . . . all of it, virtually. I think you are wherever you put yourself at the time, because that's where you want to be. People do it to pass the time, like writing a book – I think that's sheer fantasy.

"There is a fantasy I have that I haven't been able to tell him . . . not yet. It's because I feel so guilty. It's about fucking my son . . ."

MARIE- ANNE

I'd just about given up on Marie, when the door-bell rang and she hurried in apologizing about being so late. She explained that she'd been shopping, was very stoned, "so you know how difficult it is to get anything together."

The first thing one notices about her is a domination of tits – a tight shirt over Levi hot pants – a veritable Heffner-delight. She has an undistinguished face, rimless spectacles over brown eyes under brown hair and is obviously conscious of her body. Her movements are nervous

A young American spaced-out traveller; she's been to the East, and other countries, and proud of the fact. Being well travelled is a status symbol for her.

Recently arrived from California she's staying in a damp basement where a bunch of young Americans live together inexpensively.

She went into her fantasy 'problem' directly. Having degrading fantasies and just simply not being able to get off without them, preoccupies her; and she obviously devotes much time to the problem.

She comes from middle-class American Jewish background; scholarly parents (her mother is a teacher, father an economist); she's been to university, has a minor degree in History of Art, which she really wasn't at all interested in.

She didn't like New York and wanted to live in Los Angeles, where she met a man who took her round the world. It was a bad experience, she said. He was an older man in his late sixties, and although she'd known that occasionally she'd have to go to bed with him, it turned out that he was very kinky, highly sexed and she became quite revolted by him. As soon as she got to Singapore she left him, continuing to travel on her own.

We talked like this for several hours. She continually projected a middle-class hippie image: digging Joni Mitchell, marijuana, Mandrax, and the Age of Aquarius philosophy. She kept saying how totally unhung-up she was about sex, how totally liberated she was; how she liked herself – so why were these fantasies necessary? And then she asked if her name had been mentioned on the tape. I said I didn't think so, but at any rate the tapes were confidential. She said good, because there was something else she had to tell me – while she had been in the East she'd been a call girl. She said she'd actually begun in New York and it was very quick easy money, so when she left the old man she was broke and decided that the best thing to do would be prostitution. There's a shortage of white women in the East and pale call-girls were very well paid and very well treated: the colour of their skin providing them with a position of superiority, she said.

As she was telling me this her personality changed. Gone was the middle-class hippie. A new woman appeared: sure of herself, louder, speedier, gayer, aggressive – she was a different person. A split had taken place. I was really amazed at the change; she'd had me totally fooled. If she'd said, I've been a whore and I had to do it because I had no bread and it was awful, I could have found a balance in that; but she didn't hate it – she spoke about it with sparkling eyes.

"Man," she said "let me tell you, it was terrific!!!" She said she really felt it was her real self, she liked the act of doing it, she liked all the things that went with it – she loves money and she liked the sweet life – no damp basements but luxury apartments with satins, mirrors, feathers; the expensive clothes, beauty salons, grooming herself, blonde wigs, taxis, maids, good food, champagne.

I had the feeling that some of the things she told me were fantasies because she certainly didn't look like that high class call girl she was describing. They sounded like the dreams a petty thief has of becoming a Mafia chief; a mousy little girl has of becoming Marlene Dietrich.

****

"I find that when a sexual situation comes up that I haven't previously thought about, or fantasized about, as groovy as it is, I can't have an orgasm. My long-term lovers have been very good ones, so I think it's me and I don't know why. The thing is, I'm not fucked up about sex particularly, I don't think. But I can't have orgasms without fantasies, I just can't. And it really hangs me up. I would much rather have one orgasm out of every four times if it was happening, by itself. I find it so disorientating, I think it's offensive – just the idea that I'm not making love with this person but that I'm involved in some other scene – like I fantasise about being fucked by an animal. And I say to myself, here I am fucking this beautiful young man, so what the hell am I doing in a zoo?

"I'm a university graduate and the only things that have ever come to me in my whole life, I mean the only good things that have ever happen to me have been because I have big tits.

"One of the things that hang me up the most is that I like my sex very gentle and I like my fantasies very violent. It's ludicrous . . . I really find it ridiculous, because I would not want any of my fantasies to happen. They're degrading and violent, nothing that I would ever tolerate in any situation of reality.

"I'm being beaten some now in my fantasies and I'm not too pleased about that because that's the only thing that could become a real possibility. I mean I'm obviously not going to be balling dogs or getting gang-raped, but *that's* a possibility.

"If only I could have a nice romantic fantasy. Do you come across women with gentle fantasies? I read somewhere that a lot of trouble women have in having orgasms is reconciling their fantasies and reality . . . there's too great a difference. Sometimes I just don't want to spoil a groovy, gentle fuck with one of my nasty fantasies, which means that I can't have an orgasm, which means that it alters the experience.

"I started late, when I was twenty, and I guess I must have had an orgasm maybe a year later when I figured out that the fantasies from masturbation would have to be carried over to this for me to be able to make it.

"After I left the old man from L.A and decided to go on the game, I met a sergeant. Sergeants are good people to hit for this because they are the highest you can get in non-commissioned officers and they know a lot of people – they've got a lot of contacts, they're always wheeling and dealing. He fixed me up. I was dating a general, a Chinese millionaire . . . I only had three Thais. Ahhh, they took me to their places, short time motels, unbelievable. Twelve mirrors round the walls, round bed, mirrors on the ceiling and a sort of thing like a modification of a stirrup in a gynaecologist's office, but all leather covered and you just lean back. And a bath tub big enough for two and piped music. Fantastic.

"I really do dig it. I cannot tell you how terrific it was. It's such a luxurious life. For a woman it's just perfumed baths and beautiful clothes and fancy restaurants and nightclubs. Oriental girls are lovely, but there are a lot of rich western men, primarily American men who want a western girl. They're mostly lonely . . . they all want love they all want affection; they all want to make love to me, very few of them want me to make love to them. I was just having so much fun doing it. I guess I didn't have many orgasms, but I wasn't looking for that. I really did enjoy it on the level of making men feel at ease and making sure they have a nice time.

"I really enjoy pleasing men; it's the only profession in the world that I'm at all cut out for. But on an emotional level I'm not able to handle it really. When men are paying you to sleep with them . . . it's obvious to feel contempt for anyone who has to pay you to be able to sleep with you. You get to dislike men. Until the past week or so I've been avoiding sexual experiences. If anybody had touched me for the last month I would have thrown up.

"One of my common fantasies is hitching – getting picked up by a lorry with about four guys in it, wearing a raincoat and not having anything underneath. Being exceedingly provocative, like masturbating myself in front of them until I go in the back with one, two o three of the truck drivers. Then I guess there's the straight *Story of O* fantasy, with some kind of very fancy skirt opened in front and just having strange men brought to me. Having to do things to them in this case. In most of my fantasies I'm doing things involuntarily.

"I've got a new one. It's so new I haven't found a good setting for it yet. Right now it's a barn, but it's not quite . . . I'm not crazy about it yet. It's balling my brother in the barn. I don't remember exactly how I got into it. There was a series of fantasies before that, my brother having seen me with somebody else, I guess. (I don't have a brother, by the way). And then him owing somebody else a lot of money and instead of paying back the money he just brings this guy over regularly and uses me as payment. And at that point it fades out into some sort of group experience, with a lot of men – which I've never done, I've done it with four people, three or four people, that's all I've ever done, but I haven't done it very often and I don't remember about fantasies then. I was so stoned at the time and the whole thing was just a dance, you know: easy, smooth, very beautiful dance.

"I no longer fantasize about women at all . . . very rarely, although I think that all my earlier fantasies were women. My first sexual experience – I was having homosexual as well as heterosexual experiences – so I was learning about heterosexual sex at the same time and I was less interested in it. And when I was about twenty-one I decided that this was the wrong trip for me to be on and I think that I really tend to absolutely avoid all homosexual experiences. Whether I would enjoy or not is irrelevant. If I can possibly avoid them, I avoid them. I don't think I'd really be completely secure in my heterosexuality until I make it without fantasies, although I really like men better than women anyway. But until I really feel secure in that, I don't want to know . . . because last time I was with a woman I remember thinking, this is better . . . better. And that's just not a reality I care to know about.

"Whether it's true or not doesn't matter to me. I really enjoy sex with men, so if I enjoy it a bit better with a woman it really doesn't matter. It's just so much more complicated.

"I try to look at every sexual experience as fun and go into it for the fun value. I'm saving some of my decadent fantasies pleasures for when I get older. For instance, I've never tried anal intercourse; you know that will be something for my thirties. What I would really like to do is fuck a big blonde. Real big blondes really drive me crazy. There's one in my yoga class – she's a model and I spend the whole class staring at her, wondering about making love to her. I'd be afraid to even approach her, but I guess I would like to. I don't know how to seduce anybody, though. I've never seduced anyone in my life.

"Oh, by the way, when I'm working I'm not Marie, I become Anne. Now I'm becoming Marie again because people are calling me Marie, and I'm reacting as Marie would react, which is entirely different than Ann would react. Anne was a groove. I like Anne much more than I like Marie, and I felt that my parents would like Anne much better, because they don't like Marie at all. They never approved of anything I did . . . like my mother found a letter in a package I sent from Singapore that said . . . I dealt some acid, I had some acid sent to me and dealt it out, and she found the letter about it, and now she's read the letter I've nothing more to say to her because she cannot possibly approve of me ever gain. And all I was ever asking is her approval.

MARY

I get to the old rambling house in Swiss Cottage in time for the lamb stew with which I could not cope as I'm a vegetarian; so I eat salads and cheese attractively laid out on pine table in the kitchen where herbs and ivy sprawl amongst the vats of homemade wine.

Her husband, David, and five teenage flower children dressed in deep velvets and satins discuss the latest events following sit-ins at the Northern London Polytechnic. Eventually the children make off and we move in front of the log fire in the unorganized sitting room where fading walls are covered in David's impressionistic paintings.

A few glasses of the wine they brew, and we are ready to begin talking about sexual fantasies. David moves to the far end of the T-shaped room to read. Mary asks him not to fall asleep as she would certainly want to make love after all the stories she would tell me. They've been married for twenty three years; he promises to be available.

They were both virgins when they married and several years later they mutually agreed to experiment with extramarital relationships; found it stimulating and continue to practice it.

Mary is a frizzy haired, slender, little published poetess. Chronologically she's middle-aged but the strong, genuine involvement with her children keeps her mind current.

She's lucid, eloquent; analytical about her fantasies which feature prominently, and almost constantly throughout her extensive sex life. She relates her strong need for their influence to the strict childhood spent in Ireland with her pious, widowed, landowning father, who crammed her with religious taboos.

****

"I'm not happy with the whole business of fantasies; because I withdraw . . . it becomes my own thing . . . totally private. Sometimes I almost forget he's there, forget to caress him and so on. But of course with David, he know they are going on and anyway he likes playing around just for his own pleasure, so it doesn't matter too much just as long as it doesn't go on too long and I get too interested in the fantasy and miss the moment that might produce the climax.

"My fantasies are nearly all of being compelled to enjoy sex. They break the inhibitions imposed on me in childhood against enjoying it.

"At first there were pretty simple things like being tied up or being carried away by an Arab prince. This latest one I consider an advance. My mind, by eventually finding the thing humorous, enabled my will to stop resisting, so that I wasn't any longer, as in earlier ones, forced into pleasure simply by the physical pleasure – the orgasm and the sensation – but actually went along with it and enjoyed the complete event, without, in this case, having to be coerced.

"The first time I had this fantasy I had a clitoral orgasm, but then I told David about it, afterwards – the next morning – so then we had another fuck and this time I didn't have a fantasy at all and I was much more relaxed than I'd ever been, and I put it down to the successful finding of a way in the story, finding a bit of truth that actually related to my true position.

"I have the deeply ingrained inhibition – which is all to do with building up dignity – that sex is totally an undignified act, and dignity has no place in it at all. This was overcome by humour in the case of this fantasy – them thinking of tickling me, or me thinking of tickling the men . . . something to break down my dignity.

"I'm a young girl married to a rich older man. He is a prince in some foreign country, so I'm completely removed from my own family. I'm there as a prisoner, only for his pleasure.

"I'm kept in a luxurious suite and I have a sort of wardress, a kind of nanny, you might say; who is affectionate, but knows her job, and her job is to keep me nice for my husband. If I misbehave I get bad marks and have to be spanked. I have to choose what to be spanked with a hairbrush, or a slipper, or an ivory cane or something like that.

"Next to the bedroom I have a very fancy bath-room with a lot of equipment – fur-lined tables for me to be laid out on, massaged, oiled, powdered, perfumed. Rugs, towels, mirrors, marble.

"On this particular evening the footman comes in with a note which he gives to my nanny. She beckons me to the bathroom, bathes me and whatnot and then she ties my feet and hands onto the table legs on which I had been lying, and I say, this is not necessary , you know, I know what I have to do. But she says it is necessary, and then the footman comes back, this time with the butler, and they start to play with me, while nanny watches and sometimes advises them on what they should do.

"They play with my nipples and round the inside of my thighs, and the butler starts the real fingering and he has a grease tube, a huge lipstick-shaped grease cake which melts on contact with the warm flesh, making it soft and oily. They play around a great deal, but they stop short of giving me an orgasm.

"Then they go away and it's all been very silent. And of course, this is why I have to be tied up. I wouldn't stand for this, to be treated like this by the servants, and I'm absolutely furious and I tell the nurse that I'm angry, but she doesn't pay attention and simply gets me dressed.

"She puts on an evening dress, with very low neck – I give myself big tits in my fantasy – with embroidery round the top, like a lady's ball dress. It's long, right down to the ground, but there's a panel at the back which can be lifted up, revealing my buttocks.

"I go into dinner and I'm sitting with the panel lifted, my buttocks on the leather seat of the chair. And the butler is there serving dinner; the footman is standing . . . maids . . . Everyone is very silent, and my husband says, I hear you didn't enjoy this evening's attention. Well, that's a shame because I have more of that kind of thing in store for you. And I start to protest and he says, never mind, eat your soup; and of course I'm feeling absolutely sick with apprehension and he's just very stern and I'm pretending to eat, but I can't eat much, I'm so nervous.

"After dinner they clear away the dishes, but not all of them; and they lay me on the table with my buttocks in the air and my husband deigns to do a bit of titillating, feeling me up, smearing oil from a cruet on me. I think it adds up to my humiliation to have a few salt cellars and half empty butter dishes still around. There's definitely something about having one's face on the white damask with knives and forks and silver vessels lying around while all this other extraordinary stuff is going on. It's the mixture of the ordinary and the extraordinary.

"Then the footman and the butler and the maids are invited to join in again, and this time the footman puts his penis in my cunt, not to come, but just to play around with it.

"They decide that I'm not really with it, and they start to tickle me, and by tickling me they make me laugh so that I break down into hysterical laughter, and then the laughter becomes genuine, I see the whole situation as hilariously funny, whereupon I lose all my dignity and go absolutely will-less and bone-less and curl up like a kitten, and they can do whatever they like and it's just completely passive and complete enjoyment."

MOLLY PARKIN

I interview Molly in her bright flat in the Chelsea Art's Club. The furnishings are eclectic – from antiques to gaudy plastics; her spacious sitting room with comfortable couches piled high with satin covered cushions overlook an enchanting garden.

She wears a voluminous, sleeveless taffeta dress, king-fisher in colour. Her jet black mop of upswept hair is held in place by three gaudily coloured metal pot scrubbers which look like strange ornaments washed up from the sea. "Got them in the market in Brixton," she explained her phenomenal head-gear. "They're for blacks, you see. The pot scrubbers you get around here are just the ordinary metal and copper ones. Mind you the copper would look wonderful in your lovely red hair." Her voice is deep, warm, gutted with experience; her accent recalls London street life.

Direct, lively blue eyes heavily rimmed with kohl, blend mystery with coyness as she takes it all in. Her generous, scarlet painted lips are renowned for witticism and 'sheer filth.' A vegetarian, she has prepared a platter of salads and cheeses for our lunch. She sips a pint of beer through three colourful plastic straws. "To keep my drinking down, you know. I was a heavy boozer, but no more. Bad for you, kid."

Though in her mid-fifties, her reputation as a femme fatal still persists. Clear to see how easy it is to fall in love with – her charisma is irresistible.

I ask her, whether, as a woman, successful writer, and femme fatal persona, did she find it better being married or living, like you do now – as a single person?

****

"I adore both. Being married because you can get on with your work. But I also love complete, irreverent promiscuity. I mean, I adore one night stands. I love casual sex – if one can manage to keep it casual. But the trouble is that I talk to them, and before I know what's happened they want my phone number: they want to see me again. Because I'm very good at talking; I'm good at making sex very easy for a person. You know there are so many people with hang-ups; it appals me how many people have awful inhibitions. I think most of it is ignorance, because we don't know, because it's always so hidden.

"I used to be awful at sex . . . until between marriages, when I was about thirty-two – that's when my first marriage broke up. That's when I went through a period of complete celibacy – you know the shock of being on your own. I felt I'd had it: I mean two small children . . .

"And then I became appalled by the number of my girlfriend's husbands, who seeing a woman on her own would always happen to be passing by and then made sexual overtures. And you know that's very difficult for a woman because those women were close friends, and it was spoiling my friendships because I couldn't tell them. But I would never sleep with their husband; that's disloyalty to a woman friend, isn't it? I hate all that.

"I thought my sexuality was finished, I really did. Who would want someone with two kids and having to get a career together . . . I had a lot of debts after my first marriage – just as I did after my second one.

"So I picked myself up and did a creative fashion job – designed hats for various trendy boutiques like Biba, and started to write about quirky fashion, and from then on I had a wonderful life: started earning a lot of money, had an au pair for the kids, and had a lot of lovers.

"Being without sex makes me very irritable, very aggressive, edgy, you know. I didn't like myself. Can't do my work well unless I have my three orgasms a day.

"I broke my celibacy spell with the milk man. One day when he came and the kids were at school and the au pair was at her language classes. He was an attractive man, you know; and in he came through the garden and I was bending over a bush of begonias, so he goosed me and I liked it and thought, why not? And so I had him and that really gave me a taste for it.

"Then started a period of intense promiscuity, like three or four lovers a day. I had a gay friend at that time – he was wonderful that friend of mine – he was the perfect companion. We cruised together and because the gay world is so promiscuous it was very exciting. But of course, a lot of the lovers I was having were not necessarily my intellectual or social equals, you know: they were just men – cocks.

"Then in a space of five years I more or less settled with three constant lovers. One was a visionary architect – and I mean like one of the best in his field – worked like Buckminster Fuller. Another was a playwright. Well I encouraged him to start writing plays. I made him leave the film production company that he was working for – changed his life: he's famous now. And the other was a topflight journalist.

"The architect would stay the night, I used to have the journalist at lunchtime and then have dinner with the playwright who then had to go back to his wife. But I also had a lot of other people too, but those three relationships were very important to me as well as for them. And I couldn't have chosen between those three men . . . and then I met Patrick.

"He came at a very emotional time of my life when my mother had attempted yet another suicide and I went to Cornwall to be near her, and I met Patrick. That was supposed to be a holiday romance, but we had one night together and we simply fell in love and in the morning he said: will you marry me Molly? I've fallen in love with you; and I said yes. He said, I'm already married, I'm having a divorce, and you're getting rid of those three lovers.

"And it happened with the first husband exactly the same way. I met him and went out with him three times and he said I want to marry you, and I said yes; because I need – I just need marriage. And I've had a lot of marriage proposals: I just get them all the time, but I don't say yes – it has to be the right person, you see it has to be the right combination. And when it's right it has to be all or nothing.

"I have very strong ideas about fidelity in marriage. This is something I've come to terms with: I can't be unfaithful in marriage. It's to do with having been brought up in such a wonderful marriage as that of my parents, as an example. And also to do with being very religious at base, I should think. You know if the church gets hold of the kid, they've bloody got you for life.

"In a committed relationship I believe in total commitment. This is why I never live with someone – 'cause I wouldn't be faithful to them: I'm only faithful when I'm a wife. I always lay it on the line – the man is not allowed to have anybody and nor am I. Marriage should have the sexual part settled, one shouldn't have to be bothered with jealousy.

"I'm just appalled by sexual jealousy because I understand it – I have a great capacity for it. I mean it's such a painful, horrible thing; I mean it makes you sick – physically sick. It's what happens when somebody you love is interested in someone else. I just cannot cope with it.

"I've punished both my husbands for their infidelity. I shall never forgive them – ever. And they love me, both these men . . . they're searching for another me. Patrick said a short while ago, where can I find another Molly? And I said never again . . .

"I understand that that first husband of mine was constantly unfaithful to me all through the marriage; and the moment I discovered his infidelity I went immediately – so I wouldn't change my mind – because I still loved him – to the lawyer. And that wasn't normal. I mean surely to Christ someone is allowed – I mean we'd been together for eleven years . . .

"Then with Patrick– I mean that jealousy that first time was un-be-lie-va-ble when I saw him – the three of us in bed – making love to what was my girlfriend! I mean she'd suggested it while we were still in Cornwall and I was appalled by the proposal. Then one night, in New York, we were all drunk and next thing I know is waking up with a lot of bodies. One was a pal of mine from a long time ago who had always wanted to score with me, and there he was screwing me. But there Patrick was . . . screwing my girlfriend! I look on the bed and there she was sucking off my husband: my love, my life, and the feeling was just horrible!

"We went off in the cab to the Chelsea Hotel and I was crying because I said: we've spoiled the marriage, we've been unfaithful. And he said: we haven't, we were in it together, and I said: we've been unfaithful. I have been and you have been and it's the end of the marriage. I knew it was. And yet we still went on a whole year more, but I could have tracked it inch by inch.

"But you know that gave me a terrific short story of course, and all that stuff. You know one does all this in one's art. And thank goodness for art because it exorcises the whole thing. But the jealousy was just unbelievable!

"One night there was a beautiful girl with a beautiful, firm, full body and silky skin. Beautiful breasts; young, she was about eighteen, and she really was very much into me and I wasn't into her, I was in despair, you know, about Patrick – our love being so defiled. And in the middle of the night he turned and started stroking me. It was dark; he thought I was the girl. He started, you know, started saying her name and how beautiful she was: stroking my breasts, thinking it was her. And he was so hot . . . and it was heart breaking, and I knew I had to stop loving him.

"And when I did manage to stop the jealousy – control it, was when eventually I killed completely that love I had for him. Otherwise I couldn't have done all those orgies; I couldn't put myself through that amount of pain. I deliberately coaxed the love out of my life. I killed it. I had to.

"I had to brace myself for those threesomes he liked. I used to dally at the bar and say, you start without me. But they didn't want to start without me, they were waiting for me – I was the catalyst. And I was crying inside, I couldn't bear it, I found those threesomes unbelievably painful.

"And then I had the boy – that was the threesome – Patrick, the boy and me. This very, very beautiful boy. I'm going to show you his photograph and then you'll understand. I mean one of the most beautiful boys in the world! And I rather did fall in love with him. In the desire to elevate myself, what did I do? Fell in love with this angel. Just to have something good and golden in my life at the time. I wasn't really in love with him, but I wanted to have an illusion of being in love. I have to have a love relationship just to show myself my soul is alive.

"And what happened was that David fell in love with the boy also . . . Ariel was his name. But he fell passionately in love with me. He was from California and he was very gentle, beautiful, sensitive outlook; and he was like my boy; like my son . . .

"We used to sleep together every night, me in the middle with those two men who were desperately jealous of each other. Like father and son. And I found it unbearable because I knew that they were suffering the same sexual jealousy of each other over me. I didn't glory in it – that was always the plight– who to choose first, who I might fuck first – you know, it's favouritism. So that I had to develop a trick of getting both their cocks, one in each cheek at the same time. And then we used to have a running joke – one of them would say to the other: do you want to put it in first? And roll over and say: it's your turn now. But underneath it was seething with sexual jealousy, and I was torn between the two of them . . .

"When Patrick had to go back to London, he cried and said: you have to make a choice between us. And I went back with him, because he was crying, and it was tearing me apart that he was crying – I cannot see a man cry. And I did leave Ariel and did choose Patrick. And as soon as we were back he started the same tricks, but still it was incredible – the sex between us.

"I suppose that what it was with my husbands is that their sex drive matched my own. Even right up to the end with Patrick, after eleven years of marriage, we were still having passionate sex three times a day. With each other, as well as the orgies. In the morning when we woke up; and because we were working together, in the middle of the day I'd feel: uh, something is missing here and I'd say to him: come on, a bit on the side of the desk; and then in the evening. We didn't have orgies every single night, except in the end . . . it was that manic. We were going to rock-bottom places, I tell you, in the desire to seek more excitement. We would go to – you know they have those screwing clubs – where the sex stars go: porn people you know; and the girls were wrecked from drugs . . . just like the last days of Babylon. A trip to Hades, and we got stuck in it.

"He was progressively wanting boys and not girls. The whole thing was a mess and I was always landed fucking the girls and I didn't want girls. I wanted Patrick, as it had been.

"And then one night we picked up these two kids and I thought: Jesus Christ, the girl is on male hormones; you know to grow muscles; and the boy is having packs on his face, to disguise the hair, and I felt that I'd been in a freak show. I'm not interested in these two, I thought. I love them but I don't want it to be my married life, and I said, it's over. He said, for Christ sakes, just shut up, it's your Puritanism again! And I went into the other room, lay on the bed, locked the door. I was awake all night and as the light of dawn hit the little trees outside my window I thought to myself: Jesus Christ, it's happened again! You're on your own, kid. Or would you rather stay in this marriage? And I thought no, some human dignity, and watched the dawn come in . . .

"In the morning he came into my room with a big erection – a big erection for me – and he said: Come on Molly, what's all this about? You've crucified my night; you're probably pleased about that. That's the first night that we've slept apart in eleven years. Well yes, I said – that's it, and isn't that an indication of something? He said: it's just that you are being spiteful, for Christ sakes. Come back to bed! And I said: I'm leaving you. What about the party tonight? You're not going to come to it? And I said, no. He said: You'd do that to me? Yes, I'm leaving you. Christ Almighty! he shouted, and that was it.

"I went to Spain. Fucking howling into the ocean, as you can imagine. He wrote to me and said I cannot ring you up to talk to you even. We were both torn apart. We were both in terrible pain but we didn't come together again. And I wrote wonderful letters to him – which I put in my memoirs, and they make everybody cry when they read them.

"I feel so damaged by those years. But it's my fault too . . . you know I was the one who pulled all those people for all those orgies because I'm much better at it than Patrick. I mean nobody forces you to do things . . . I had to go through all that shit . . . But he didn't see it as having been shit – real hell.

"I mean before I'd never been in an orgy when I loved the person. I can't share, I can't do it. There's nothing wrong with admitting that. And I've never been in an orgy where somebody wasn't using somebody. But the suffering is essential to understanding sex, and yet one tries to protect oneself against it. But you mustn't ever lose the quality to suffer. You know in all those years of orgies I was coerced and debased but never hardened. In fact quite the opposite. The suffering through the jealousy made me understand and love more. I didn't feel bitter, bitterness is destructive.

"What drew men to me, in the end, is this motherly thing I've got. I'm just wonderfully kind to them. I wouldn't turn down any man – colour, creed, beauty. I never ever turn down old men. I think that old men are wonderful. I slept with a lot of old men when I was very young – like twenty–one. We're talking about eighty-year-olds, whose sexuality matched that of Onassis, I should think. They taught me more than any of the young ones with a big cock did. And if I'm a wonderful lover, I have the benefit of the experience of those old men – although half of them couldn't get a cock-rise. They gave me wonderful come jobs . . . showed me how to touch and what to do. Friends have said to me: ugh, how could you be with those old men, and I said I love them; I simply do love them . . . in their frailty. Looking down on bald heads just filled me with this incredible rush of love, tenderness . . . and for them to have a young girl was a wonderful gift. Boys now offer themselves to me as a gift, and it's a very sweet thing to do. The youngest that I had was sixteen . . . sweet as a nut he was.

"I've never been able to understand my sexual appeal. It's like a sort of aura, isn't it? The more sex you have, the more lovers you have, you pull. It's like with everything, nothing succeeds like excess! I suppose I am a femme fatale, but I don't mind . . . I don't know, because I'm not a beautiful woman and the body's seen better days.

"One of my lovers said to one of my other lovers: I don't know what it is about Molly, this incredible pull she's got on men. She's a short, tubby, ugly little runt, with eyes all rimed in kohl and hair completely wrecked by chemicals, but she's got the same sort of sexual appeal as Edith Piaf's.

"I think the thing is really – and this might be a clue to my rampant sexuality – that deep down I'm very frightened and shy, and all this is exhibitionism – all the clothes and hats is a way of getting people to look at that – the persona, not me. I'm really hiding myself. So the thing of having to pull – though I'm not desperate to do it – is about power. I have to have the power of knowing that I can pull.

"But I don't get much of it anymore. I mean if I stopped now I've had enough to last me for the rest of my life. Now I can use sublimation for my three orgasms a day. I've got my *Angel's Delight*, I've got the vibrators, all of that I've got. And if I don't have a man in my bed to go to sleep with, well I also like not having company. I like very much to be on my own – it's a wonderful luxury going to sleep on one's own: ah, a little music, reading, very quiet: seeing to yourself. But when I'm doing that, I always have a little plastic egg in me. You see you put it in and it just gently vibrates inside you. I go to sleep with this little egg in me – it costs me a lot in batteries.

"Probably because I've lived out so many sexual experiences I don't have too many sexual fantasies. I've explored almost all the avenues of sex, I can't think of anything I haven't done that I want to do. I have tied people up and been tied up myself, and have sort of sadomasochistic relationships with people . . .

"Mind you I do fantasize about being a high class courtesan. I like the idea of charging for it: I would like to be paid. There was a very wealthy aristocrat absolutely obsessed with me. He gave me a 1932 Rolls Royce. I have a thing about cars. Cars are very important to me and I'm not talking about fucking Rolls Royce's; I'm talking about the era of the car – I've never had an ordinary car. The car is a sex symbol. It explains a person's attitude to life; and if they've got a saloon car they are interested in safety – in a suburban house with a mortgage . . . I could never go out with a man who drives a Ford. Or I couldn't be with a man whose car breaks down: impotent fucker. I understand about running out of petrol, but . . .

"Anyway, I was living in this yellow house and he gave me a yellow Rolls Royce and I said: take it back, I don't want it, it's the wrong colour. He'd already given me a yellow Morgan sports car, so I had the yellow sports car out there, and I said: I don't like the Rolls – wrong colour!

"I only fucked him once, and I said I'm charging you for it – a thousand quid. And I want it all in notes, I said, half before and half after. So he said: I'll give it all to you before; and I said: that's not the rules; they're my rules and I'm telling you! He was so excited and he was a hopeless fuck, he just really came the moment he came near me. And I talked filth to him . . ."

MONA

The small, green car insisted: honk, honk, honk as I was skipping down the King's Road, blissed out because it was a sunny day finally after many weeks of London-greyness. Realizing that the hooting could be for me, I looked around, and heard Mona's laugh behind the lowered windscreen.

Mona – twenty-two-years old, black American from New York has limpid jade eyes which she has bestowed on the daddy-less-son. Part time actress she deals dope to supplement her meagre Social Security check to which she's entitled as an unwed mother.

"Hi," I call out. "Come have coffee, tea, maybe get high. I just bought a new tape; come tell me your fantasies."

****

"A friend was supposed to come over and fuck me this morning. He didn't show. I was so bugged. I had a douche . . . got myself pretty . . . put the baby to sleep . . . and he didn't come!!! He phoned, but he didn't come.

"When I grew up I can remember my parents balling. I was eight or nine . . . very aware in that direction. But I already used to try and fuck the little boy downstairs, at four or five. My mother would go to the store and he'd rush up.

"But my first orgasm must have been when I was eight. He played with my clitoris and this beautiful sensation came over me. I can remember it very clearly . . . because I didn't have another one till I was twenty-one!!!

"My mother found us fooling around in the hall and she really . . . she really laid into me . . . which was the wrong thing to do. It really fucked me up at the time. Probably still fucking me up!!!

"My parents used to ball most evenings . . . most times . . . and I used to lie awake in the other room listening . . . listening. Then I stopped doing that because it bugged me . . . probably because I couldn't do it too. The last time they were here they were balling. My place is very small. They stayed with me . . . and they'd hide away when I was asleep . . . when they thought I was asleep.

"It was actually much different from what I imagined it to be. I didn't see them, but I could hear them. Usually when someone is balling you go to sleep, but my mother and father!!!! It freaked me a bit . . . maybe because I'd just had the baby and didn't have an old man. My mother was very stoned on Mandrax, and my father had been smoking a lot of shit. They are heads, you know, so are very natural, very open. Very young.

"My mother had me when she was fifteen. She's very pretty, small, black chick. Lively. My father is handsome . . . tall. He's a nice cat; he's just really from the old school. He's groovy . . . a musician, a head, an alcoholic, and he makes good bread. He's a bit of an asshole actually. For instance I've got two very groovy American girlfriends, and they're into what else everyone else is into . . . balling . . . touching . . . grooving . . . holding. Not being up-tight about it. So we went walking down the Portobello Road one beautiful sunny day and they were very stoned and my Dad was very stoned and they put their arms around him and all he could do was act like some sort of . . . yeah, instead of taking it cool and enjoying it, he was making smart comments like hmmmmmmmmhmmmmm baby, hey baby, hmmmm.

"I thought, why is he coming on like this? He's embarrassing me!!!! I don't really see how he turns my mother on . . . I'm really disappointed in her. Although he probably gives really good head. In fact, that's what she told me, she said, I've put up with twenty five years of shit and the only thing this man can do for me is give me some head. Oh wow!!!

"You should see the size of my son's prick. Wow, what's he going to do to some poor chick when he lays his eyes and that on her!!! He's going to get into all sorts of things that one, at a very early age.

"Kids get into whatever they want to get into because they are very aware. Much more than adults think. I know that when my aunt's boyfriend came into the bathroom while I was having a piss, I wanted to touch it, and did touch it. But my thought was, is he going to want me always to touch it when he's alone with me because I'm not always gonna want to. This at five! And thinking, will he tell my mother? And I couldn't reason that of course the son of a bitch wouldn't tell my mother!!! So I touched it and you know it made me very paranoid for a while, because I was afraid someone else is going to find out. It's the fucking guilt thing. And I don't want men to do that with children. It's only men who usually make trips like that – with children – because their fantasies are somewhat else all together. Different category!!!

"My father, the last time I saw him kind of planted this kiss on me which wasn't fatherly at all . . . but actually I'm sure he didn't know what he was doing. I sort of took the kiss, feeling tongue in my mouth, but I didn't really respond. I stood shocked, thinking, oh fuck! What was that all about?

Got uptight for a minute, then I shrugged my shoulders and said, that's groovy. I wonder how he'd feel about my fantasy? Sometimes I've been tempted to tell my mother about it.

"It must have started when I was about fifteen. I realized once again that they were balling with their door closed. I'd go into the room afterwards, get to smell the odour, the muskiness . . . things like that. I began wanting to be in that room with them. I began seeing them making love while I was making love with some cat . . . and then interchanging in my mind, and balling my mother . . . feeling her smooth tits . . . kissing them . . . touching her cunt . . . making her clitoris hard . . . and having someone else in the room getting into my father. A cat getting into his arsehole . . . my father giving him head . . . and then the other person goes, splits, and we all just have this beautiful, slow, sexual thing. My mother, my father and me . . . just balling each other . . . my father on top of me . . . on top of my mother . . .my mother giving me head . . . me being my mother jerking my father off. "

MONICA

I get the impression of speed and activity around Monica. Aware, unselfconscious, direct, sensual. She has been living with Norman, a successful twenty-nine year old scriptwriter, for five years. Their circumstance is one of middle-class comfort, intellectual stimulation, sociability. They have a two year old son, Mark.

Their large, friendly, airy, expensive house in Camden Town overflows with guests on the afternoon I talk to her. There's an eighteen year old girl baking brown bread in the Habitat kitchen; a young man on the wood staircase simultaneously playing the mouth organ and guitar; an American woman who is in London for a female lib. conference, discusses socio-political patterns with another house guest, a psychoanalyst from Paris, in the spacious, uncluttered sitting room.

We conducted the interview in the sunny, white bedroom on the queen-size mattress on the floor amongst scattered toys and the baby son sleeping in his cot.

Born in a Welsh village, she lived there until at the age of eighteen she was given a grant at a college in Hounslow. She did a secretarial course for a year, loathed it; didn't have any relationships with men during that time. Finally borrowed money from her elder brother and went to France where she had an affair, the only man she'd been to bed with until she met Norman.

She returned to London, worked for the London School of Economics as a field secretary and shortly after starting the job she met her husband.

I'm not sure if they give each other much affection: she never mentioned love for Norman in the interview, all the love she talked about was for her son.

****

"I never knew, I still don't know what being good in bed meant. I used to imagine it as knowing techniques: weird and wonderful ways of stimulating men either with your hands or twisting the body and doing things with the muscles of your cunt. I know you can cross your legs and it's something to do with your pelvic bones . . . it's as if you want to pee very badly. If you can fuck this way it causes the man immense pleasure. Maybe it's not just not being hung up about sex; which I certainly don't feel I am.

"I knew about fucking when I was six. We lived in a village in Wales and it seemed to me that all the kids were fucking at that age, and they kept it quiet so it was obviously something which was forbidden. I thought it was something that kids in my village just did, so I had my first sexual experience when I was seven and I remember being told afterwards that somebody had fucked me, but looking back on it maybe they didn't and they were just playing. I don't remember the sensation of having anything inside me, but I certainly enjoyed it.

"I didn't do it again until I left home and went to university. I never had a boyfriend in my home environment, I knew it was impossible. I would never make up or try to look attractive. I couldn't in anyway be in sort of sexual competition with my mother for my father.

"My mother was psychotic, but her psychosis was sexual jealousy – she thought everyone was fucking my father, including her children. That is what hit me when I was in adolescence. It hit me at my most vulnerable moment, so in a way I can't understand why I'm not totally hung up sexually. I never was hung up sexually at all – I never believed in marriage, I always believed that if you liked somebody you should sleep with them and I couldn't understand why you shouldn't. But I'm not forward in anyway. I was always extremely shy with boys: the moment they would look at me in the street I blushed horribly red. I'm not promiscuous. I've only slept with one other man than Norman.

"I've always had a very pure attitude towards sex. I never laughed at dirty jokes – I thought they were smutty and I realized that people were telling them because it was based on their ignorance.

"I see sex very much as a form of expression. I still think it's better that you should like somebody, but also if you don't like anybody why should you go without it? But at the moment I wouldn't fuck anybody else mainly because I would be afraid of hurting Norman . . . but if we came to some sort of agreement about it then I would. But we really haven't come to any solution. I think we both feel that if you start fucking someone else you might prefer that person, you might want to go with them; you might split up. But I mean when I'm fucking I'm very rarely fucking him.

"I'm surprised that you say that a lot of women don't have fantasies when they're fucking. I heard that it was very common, that it applied to almost all women. That all the time they conjure up images while they're fucking. I mean, that's what I do, I do it all the time. I don't dwell on my fantasies after fucking.

"I think I have a few sexual fantasies outside of when I'm fucking. I wouldn't say they don't exist, but it's when I'm fucking that I fantasize all the time. I wonder, when you say lots of women don't, what is in their minds at the time. It's not that I fantasize to get an orgasm, because I can usually achieve orgasms very, very quickly and many, many orgasms; and I feel sometimes quite angry because he has ejaculated and I've only had five orgasms and could go on for another ten years. At other times I don't care whether I've had an orgasm and maybe I'm tired. So I don't think I'm using fantasy as a way of achieving orgasm. My experience of orgasm is climbing the top of a hill or a mountain or something. When I reach an orgasm, I sometimes . . . it comes out of my head and I relate it to something quite ordinary like doing the housework in the daytime and I'm experiencing the orgasm with that — with something that I've been doing. It's something as ordinary as sweeping the floor, which can become very exciting. Like I find green peppers — maybe red peppers also — extremely erotic. You open them up and find that little ball of white seeds . . . I find it extremely arousing. Sometimes I get so aroused that I turn around and have to throw the whole thing into the bin — the seed thing, not the pepper. I feel when I touch them, all tingle all through my fingers, I can feel it now just thinking about it . . . feel all those seeds . . . you just play with all these seeds. And when I'm fucking I'm very much aware sometimes of wanting to spread seed as far as possible . . . with my body. You know, my movements while I'm coming, it's all like I'm trying to spread the seed as far as possible.

"I have fantasies about being fucked by animals, because what I want is to be fucked by a huge penis. Either by a bull or by a horse. A horse, because I read that in Persia they have shows where they tie up a donkey and they have a girl . . . I don't know how they do it, but they do something to make the penis . . . somehow they get it in. And I once saw a horse with a very erect penis . . . and I imagine myself on all fours and this huge penis fucking me.

"It's not a flash . . . it's not a scene . . . it's just an act. I'm fucking it. It's not so much the pressure of its body, but the big penis, always the big penis. That's why I have fantasies about fucking Negroes; they have the big penis, bigger than white men . . . which I know is a myth.

"Usually my fantasies relate to real experiences. I remember when I was fifteen, it was summer and I was at home and we had this dog. I didn't know anything about the sex life of a dog, but he was obviously very heated up, going around with whining and his paws all close together, with his body arched and his penis hanging down. At the time I was feeling very sexy — I mean it was years before I had any sex relations — and I really wanted to push the dog on top of me. I mean, I might have tried had I not worried about upsetting that dog.

"I very much like to get fucked in an animal position – you know, on all fours. With the man coming in from behind you it's also a way of getting the penis right inside, and that's how we fucked a few minutes before I went into labour. Maybe there's a connection – my animal fantasies and wanting to fuck my son. Freud said the most perfect love was the love between a mother and her baby son, because the mother has got her penis and this love is very important to the child. This is the greatest love affair of your life because you have got somebody totally and any subsequent love affair is just the shattered fragments of this first great love affair. But it follows that the better the original love affair with your mother the better your love affairs and, in fact, not just love affairs, but relationships during your life, are going to be. I very much have this in mind. I wonder how much that enables me to have fantasies about Mark, without having any guilt about it. If you honestly believe in that, you know that the proper thing is to have a good love affair with your son."

ROINA

Roina is from a socially unprivileged background. She had a nervous breakdown and spent several months in two different mental institutions. At twenty-three she looks at least five years older, but has a soft, generous, open face. She talks speedily. Her proclivity is for black men – for years she hasn't slept with a white man – but there is no guilt attached to her specific appetite). They are good together. The problem for them comes from a society which doesn't accept them. From the white people and from the black people as well.

****

"So many people write about sex. More probably about sex than anything else. The thing is, it's so limitless . . . because people are so different, you know.

"I dig spontaneity. I can't stand just going to bed and every night the same and same again; it drives me up the wall. I just like to be doing the washing up or something like that and bang! He takes me right from behind. Or suddenly just racing out to the woods; or in the park or anywhere . . . Once I did it in a graveyard; that was nice. A little bit tipsy on cider and lying amongst all those creepers and being given head on a tomb . . . it was really good.

"I really dig my breasts being kissed and touched and things like that. If a guy doesn't do that, like, I feel a bit insulted

"Occasionally guys just want to fuck me, you know; just wanna fuck, and not care about it. It just pisses me off . . . I feel it's a sort of an insult. I like it to be a two way thing because it's very nice then.

"What I dig when I'm fucking actually is that I like being talked to. All sorts of talk, dirty and loving. Also the man's orgasm excites me very much.

"The guy I'm going out with at the moment – not the Jamaican I've been going out with a long time – the other guy, the one from Nigeria – he takes quite a long time to come. I've never met anyone like him actually; when he comes he really does make a lot of noise. He makes more noise than most guys I remember . . . it's more like a woman when he comes . . . I find that very exciting.

"Finally I got it together now; it's taken me . . . what? I'm twenty-two and I lost my virginity at sixteen; so it's taken me that long!

"What happened when I lost my virginity was that I was very disappointed, and I even said so to the guy, you know. I just turned around to him and said: "My God, is that all?" I was only sixteen; I didn't have any cool at all. And I got pregnant straight away, actually. We only did it about once . . . I had very ironic sort of luck, or fate. So anyway he left me straight away because he just wanted to make me pregnant.

"Then I went with another guy that I'd met when I was fifteen. And *he* told me I was frigid, so this laid it all on my mind when I was pregnant.

"Then I had the baby, and then I thought I was frigid all the time. And I felt that I was having a child and I didn't know anything about sex and I felt very cheated.

"So, anyway, what happened to me was I thought: I'm frigid, I can't live if I'm frigid, so I sort of screwed two or three guys and got V.D. Anyway it didn't prove that I wasn't frigid.

"So I phoned up one of my friends; "I'm going to a doctor, I can't stand it!" "Oh my God," she said "come over and talk to me." She said: "Men are really not that good. I never have an orgasm."

"So I went to see her and we had a really good chat, and that was the start of talking about it – when I was seventeen. So then I realized there really wasn't anything wrong with me. And then I went out with a guy who was very ignorant, but very basic, and I had my first orgasm with him. But he wasn't through to my head at all, you know what I mean, but just the physical part of it was very sort of earthy

"Like my own fantasy trip is a basic, idealistic, primitive, earthy existence – men and children; away from cities and things like that. This is my real, ultimate fantasy. A house in the country, not England – somewhere abroad, away. Things like having food to eat, having a bed to sleep in . . . having a roof over my head and having a man that I dig to be with. It's enough, I don't need money – I need enough to get by and no more. I'm hopeless with money. I'm terrible; I've got no money value at all. If I ever get money I spend it, that's all there is to it. I spend it . . . You see I've been poor for so long . . .

"I come from a low-income bracket background, yeah. I come from a working-class Irish Catholic family. They were both peasants, very, very poor, with no shoes in the winter, all that sort of thing.

"My mother's quite intelligent academically, but she's very naive about life. My father's not so intelligent academically. He works this boiler house but is very experienced in life. And so they both even out. They both argue a lot but they both wouldn't know what to do without each other. Pretty human, except in relationship to certain things like hippies, and . . . black men; which they don't approve of, but that's just their . . . otherwise they are pretty human people.

"They have a pretty fucked up sex life. They don't sleep together. It hung me up tremendously. We don't bring up sex in our family. I'm the only one that ever brings it up, and believe me, it's difficult, but I get to such a point that I have to.

"And I've tried to speak to my mother about her situation, but she won't. You know, she loves me very much, she's very demonstrative. My father finds it more difficult.

"My father is certainly the master in the house. My mother nags him a lot but she wouldn't cross his path really. So I've always had a very dominant male figure in my life, and I do go for very dominant men, and all that crap you know.

"But I've always got my way, I was always difficult, you see – because of my father. I could always twist him around my little finger; I always got my own way. Even when I was a little kid I used to attempt suicide' you know; and I failed – melodramatically – just to get my way.

"I had a very sexual thing about my father when I was younger. My mother was very jealous of me She became jealous of me when I reached puberty and I picked it up straight away, and we argued and have argued ever since.

"I left home at seventeen, after I had my kid, because I was just arguing every day, and I was getting very violent with her, you see, smashing the place up and . . . Which is something I've never done with anybody else. I never argue with the boyfriends I like, because I don't like any hassle.

"I had the baby adopted. I could trace him, because by mistake I've got their names: the Court sent me the wrong paper – bureaucratic boob! You know, I regret it. I could trace him, but I never would. He's too old now. I basically, subconsciously, feel guilty, for giving him away. And this was tied down with my illness . . .

"I had a break down . . . just lost interest in life, let myself go. You know, you can't be bothered with yourself, your physical appearance . . . I had a sort of, inability to eat; in a sense that you really have to force the food down, because it's the only way to stay alive.

"I had a personality disorder, very extreme behaviour, always very indecisive. I was crying all the time. I was filled with this tremendous sadness . . . I would walk along the street and feel so sad and cry . . . I wouldn't care who saw me, I would see the sadness in other people . . . I couldn't see any happiness at all, I couldn't see any light, it was like a big bottomless pit. I just kept swallowing pills and crashing out . . . you know.

"Then I suddenly thought, wow, I can't handle this – I gotta get away, I gotta get away from my environment and everything, you know; so I just took off to the Canary Islands with about five shillings in my pocket and this spade that I'd known a couple of years. He was a friend and I felt happy. I got on a boat and when we got near to the south – farther away from England and the February weather, and things . . . I thought, wow! And I felt the sun and the wind in my hair and I laughed, and felt good and I went and I wrote my first poem called Happiness. And I've never looked back from there even though I've had a lot of bad things happen to me. But they were nothing, those sorts of things, they were just things I had to live through and get over . . . so called bad situations. I nearly got murdered in Spain, and I got raped twice. By two American negroes.

"I can dig the rape thing – the semi-rape thing. I tie it up with religion, you see, because there's masochism in Catholicism. I'm not saying only Catholics say this, because women have this masochistic streak in them. I can dig that to an extent; but I can't say that when I was raped, I liked it. I should have just dug it, but I just didn't dig the guys at all, you know, so I couldn't get into it.

"I have a lot of fantasies when I'm not fucking. I might be working or something and I find it very boring, you see, so I just loon off . . . Or I might see somebody on the tube . . .

"I think that in fantasy you can have everything you want and need. Your mind is so vast, so fantastic and so intricate that there is always something that you can trip out on. Because it's an escapism that is important. I believe it's a very important part of the female makeup, to be able to do this, to be able to escape, I mean. The bored housewife, for example. She shouldn't be a bored housewife, but there are bored housewives, and because there are, they should be able to escape this boredom . . . at least some of the time . . .

"It's a substitute for something. I think it's a physical part of our lives and I think if you need to fantasize at a certain period more – it's like if you need to masturbate more – it's your need and you should do it. You shouldn't deny yourself.

"I make up elaborate stories, sexual stories, and really turn myself on. In Spain I met this Berber, this basic, passionate mountain man, and I used to fantasize sexual scenes with him, like . . . We are coming from the Canary Islands to the mainland and we get really drunk one night, and so he tells his girl-friend to piss off and he comes into my cabin and I just look at him and say I want to kiss you, you know, because I don't care about being the initiator so I just say, oh kiss me, and he really kisses me – the Berbers are just sort of sex crazy , and we go up and have it in the life boat. And when we get off there are people watching us, and this turns me on, as we're doing all sorts of things to each other. And then we go downstairs and do it under the shower and because we had been drinking, it takes him ages to come.

"I was really fucking sore – I could hardly stand it – it was so good. And he drags me off and says: I must have you again, and he drags me off to this town in the south of Spain (I should have been on my way to London) and we go onto the beach and we nearly get ourselves shot through sex. They patrol the beaches and they shoot anybody in sight because they don't have anybody to answer to.

"And then after we've done it on the beach, and oh, I can hardly walk, about three in the morning we climb up these sorts of slopes and we find ourselves right in this person's front garden. And the lights are shining on everything and we just had it on their lawn and it was really great, and he goes up my arse and I'm saying please, look I can't stand it , I really can't, no, but he insists and he was really big , really so passionate . . ."

SAGITTARIAN

Sagittarian, born in California is twenty-one years old. She has a small income which gives her freedom to travel and has been on the road now for three years. At present she's taking a break in London, to assimilate her experiences; but intends to continue travelling, assuming various roles and to do many things intensely.

Tall, strong charming girl whose vulnerability shows through her assumed worldliness, she's into brown rice and large quantities of home-made bread.

She has chocolate-colour, observant lively eyes; wears an Indian silk scarf round her long, fair hair; a patchwork shirt she made herself, a soft, blue skirt to her ankles, and cowboy boots come rain or shine.

She paints delicate pastel pictures of flowers; composes songs; is selective about who she goes to bed with and searches for someone to tell her truths as she walks briskly, laughs loudly, smokes a lot of marijuana and takes acid.

When she was nine her parents were divorced, which was a traumatic jolt in her comfortable, middle-class American upbringing.

She was late for our appointment as she met a young man in a music shop where she was buying strings for her guitar.

****

"My father used to race cars a lot. He was an ex-playboy from a very wealthy family. He was spoiled; very handsome. So charming. He's never settled down, always goes looking for another race, you know. Blow anything that he was into and just go. Which I thought was wonderful and I was behind it all the time. He had a dark-red Ferrari and we used to go tearing around . . . I was a speed freak too . . . we would almost get lost in speed; my father and I. This would be the only time we would be together because I wasn't so good at home. So he would take me out driving. We would stop and talk and I'd missed him so; and I would snuggled up to him and he'd put his arms around me and wherever we went I was his girlfriend. This was my father and I'd think of him as my lover . . . which I'd really felt, but it was a thing I didn't realize. But my father recognized it. I remember that I seemed an embarrassment to him one night, and I knew there was something he was afraid of. And I'd start kissing my father, and my poor father would get so turned on and he'd say, now Sagittarian, hey Sagittarian . . . and I'd just be kissing him . . . adoring him. Kissing his ears, mouth, his eyes, and he would kiss me, and we would kiss maybe for half an hour. God, my father must have gotten so turned on. But he never came onto me, never like fondled my breasts, or did anything that I would have been afraid of . . . no, maybe I wouldn't have been afraid . . . he probably should have.

"I went to Hollywood when I was seventeen and met my true love there. He was gentle and lovely and soft – a Moon-Child – and it had been a long time since I felt, well here is my soul. He was so lovely and passive, very slender, graceful like a swan. People would watch him when he walked because he floated. They way he would sit would put me to shame. I loved to watch him smoke . . . his hands . . . He was like a prince, well he is, he's got to be a prince. I would almost try to annoy him in a way, so that he would be strong and forceful. I wanted to be . . . not brutalized, but I wanted . . . like you would imagine a king to be with his court girls.

"Fantasy? Sometimes it's impossible to distinguish the real from the dream . . . that is, if you believe a distinction exists. I had a lover in my head once. We made beautiful love . . . just beautiful. You know how sex goes into different trips. Every time I have sex I'm a mother, I'm a lover, I'm savage, very savage like a jungle-woman, and then very innocent, very childlike, very sexy, very weak, very strong.

"I'll tell you a fantasy of mine because I've been thinking about it a lot . . . it's very weird . . . about a lover . . . he made me come without ever having been able to touch me.

"I ran away with the gypsies, right. It had been so long since I'd been in touch with anything that felt real, right, and I just went completely into . . . a very unwritten story . . . it just hadn't been chronicled yet . . . then. A manner of living . . . a life through green valleys with songs, bathing in rivers, being dried by the sun like lazy lizards on blue rocks. Developing such closeness with the soil that I used to rub garlic on me . . . squeeze the juice into my plastic, asphalt saturated pores. Smells had to be from the bottom of the moist earth . . . earth, dirt, mud, grass-stained wardrobe that you wrap around yourself.

"There was the King of the Gypsies. He would wear white leather and one of those images around his neck, and with a lot of black hair. He would sing these incredible songs, play his guitar and be mystical. He would ride bareback on this black horse, with such force, hunger, life, even violent life; with such incredible speed through the trees, and he would remind me of my father, in his dark–red car.

"We saw each other from the very beginning of the trip. From afar. There was a lot that stood between us. A lot of . . . I won't say classes, but you know, we weren't at all to meet like this. As far as this journey was going, it was our destiny to take different roads to make this voyage as it was supposed to be. We just saw each other.

"Very late at night, after travelling maybe a couple of hundred miles, with so many people, children, animals; and cooking our dinner and playing music, I would leave the campfire and like go walking . . . chasing stars . . . dreams.

"And I would find him in my mind, the beautiful King of the Gypsies who laughed like my beautiful father, and there was this incredible, huge, tie-dyed tepee, and it was just put on the wet grass which was about two feet high and very cold. And I had this huge long cape I'd throw down.

"In my fantasy we would fall down or we would . . . he would undress me and I'd be standing in my cowboy boots. I had been living in my cowboy boots for a long time and I'd always related . . . they're just part of me, so they fit into a lot of my fantasies.

"And he wore those incredible long white leather pants. We would start making love, and it was very cold so he would wrap me up in this big, huge wool cape, and we would make love in the tepee and with my dreams of him I'd build such energy . . . of fucking . . . just fucking, real fucking. He would be my energy, he would eat my inside, but he wouldn't be violent; he was . . . when he was on that wild black horse it was as though he was trying to break out of the womb, it was as though he was going to suffocate. Unless he made it out, he might not, you know.

"And then in the tepee on the cold grass I was on the horse with him and the speed felt like driving with my father when I was a little girl. And I'd be on this horse totally naked except for the cowboy boots. Beautiful horse, very smooth, very . . . very big – and we were riding bareback, going down an archway . . . long . . . long . . . as far as I really could see. Through an archway built of trees . . . through an arbour.

"We were running very fast, the temperature like an ice-blue-secret . . . cool and damp, but there's sun all around and we are going so fast and the only thing I can see beyond is a meadow of trees, under us all green grass, and then this orchard; and all these apple trees in bloom. And I come through it so fast until there is no man or horse any longer and I'm just floating through this orchard and it changes from ice-blue to like pink clouds, and I'm sailing along on them.

"My whole body is taken up from my pelvis, all my energy is right here, and its light as pink clouds, and I'm fucking pink clouds. Then I explode into a colour kind of trip . . . in chaparral colours. Colours going all out and around me, like a peacock.

"But it's not just visual . . . I can *feel* it . . . I feel very pink and soft, like clouds. The feeling just overcomes everything . . . and I'm sailing through nothingness . . . just nothingness, even my lungs are affected. They become very airy and spearmint. Very cool, like a rushing river . . . and I come."

SALLY

Thick-calved, legs primly crossed at the ankles, Sally sits tucked on a small settee near the narrow window framed by whit chintz curtains, which overlooks a grey wire-fenced, muddy, uneven, grassless square where a gang of loud little boys tug at a swing made of slashed truck tires.

Twenty-seven, long dark hair, dull blue eyes carefully made up; she wears a yellow frock bought at the local high-street market.

Passive and shy, she offers me milky, sugar-laden tea and biscuits from a family size Woolworths' box.

The two rooms flat in Acton is crowded with commonplace, catalogue furniture. On the wall above the bordered fireplace hangs a print of blue horses galloping through a stormy field, bought during an excursion to Blackpool.

She was born in the borough; got a secondary modern education at the local grammar school and now works at the Post Office down the road. A trip to the West End is special.

Her thirty- year- old husband works for twenty pounds a week in a factory near Twickenham and drives a small, second-hand car. They go to the pub on Saturday night; lunch with her parents on alternative Sundays, then go to the pictures. They have one-hundred-and-fifty pounds in the Post Office savings.

The furthest she's been from home is the Isle of Wight; would like to go to Spain even though she hears that the food is no good and the water gives you a bad stomach.

Ritually they watch television in the evening; go to bed at eleven and get up to the chimes of the automatic tea-making apparatus at seven.

****

"I've just had one man in my life and this is what I regret and always have. I think variety is the spice of life – you've got to compare, really, and then settle down.

"I think you get bored with one man when you've only had one man. Is that unusual or something? I find I'm getting bored. He's a good husband, I feel guilty sometimes . . . but I wouldn't mind knowing someone else.

"I was twenty-one when I got married and I was a virgin up till then. You see, seven years ago it made a big difference. Quite honestly there wasn't the pill then . . . but nowadays sexual freedom is nothing. You know what I mean? Let's put it this way – all the girls I know, they all seem to know much more about men then I did at their age.

"They've all got stories to tell. I mean these days women seem to get as much out of it as men, don't they? Girls just have a better time of it altogether. Six or seven years ago . . . it's amazing how time is different.

"Then it was considered man's pleasure, wasn't it? Even the men today, you see, they've got the girls for free, and the men know so much more. Things you see on television . . . the men are so much better . . . much better . . . more exciting. I have visions of everyone going to bed with everyone else . . . just knowing it all.

"My husband doesn't know very much about women. It doesn't worry him that much, but I wish it did. That's probably why I have these dreams.

"And yet he's all talk. When he's out in a crowd George is the loudest, George is all blah, blah, blah when we go out. We've had rows over this.

"It may sound ridiculous, but I don't think you see enough naked men. You know you get women splattered about everywhere and yet you never get men, and I think this is wrong. I mean you can't compare the man's part of the body.

"We went to the pictures the other night and you saw both the man and the woman. I don't know whether you saw the film – I forget what it's called, but you saw the man. Well I even said to my husband, he's big there, isn't he? And I noticed he was a lot bigger than my husband there. I wondered what it would be like with him; would I get a better orgasm with him being bigger? I think seeing films like that excites you . . . it does me anyway.

"I'm always thinking of other men. You see, you hear the girls talk and they say, this one's good, the other's no good, and I imagine myself with someone else. And it's always comparing someone that's much better than my husband . . . someone who's got a way with him.

"I suppose because I don't know many men that I imagine things about them – their experience and knowing it all. Say, if I had a man caller it would cost me a thought you know . . . if they made advances at me. I can imagine myself with the man with the Hoover . . . or I watch television and think about some fellow and think he's so nice that fellow . . . just look at him.

Sometimes my husband brought photographs home. They usually just pass them around at work . . . you get all that sort of thing in factories . . . mostly from the coloured blokes. Well they've got all this thing going about coloured men, haven't they? Some say once you've been with a coloured man you won't go with white men. They're supposed to be very much bigger, and they talk longer to excite a woman. I've heard so much about it that I believe it, but whether it's true or not, I don't know. And I've seen some beautiful looking girls with them and I think, you know, it must be true. I think if they're bigger they must be better.

"But I always think about Frank Sinatra. I've read about him, you know, and he's had so many women, he's a proper ladies man. I should imagine he's quite something. He's so handsome. He knows it all . . . how to stimulate a woman. I pretend that we're out in the country . . . it's nowhere where I live at all . . . and with him I imagine it's totally different. He's much more affectionate and everything else and touches me all over and I'm much more excited, ever so excited with him, and we make love in different positions and he plates me, and I feel very beautiful, much more stimulated than I ever am with my husband, and his orgasm is much, much bigger than my husband's, and the orgasm I have with Frank Sinatra is just something fantastic."

TERESA

Teresa is forty and married to Adrian, five years her senior. He's an avant garde playwright who earns substantial sums of money on some of his screen-plays that get made into films.

Although on the previous occasions when I'd met him (which includes visits to my house with bunches of tulips) he was always charming, inquisitive and amusing, but today he was antagonistic because I was interviewing his wife on her sexuality. He said he wasn't angry because she was talking to me ("to you, dear") but because she never gave 'him' material for his plays.

They live in a cottage near Cambridge and the atmosphere in the house is highly active – an intellectual set-up. Books, papers, manuscripts, letters, strewn on the living room table, shelves, chairs and floor.

Adrian struts in and out of the comfortably furnished living room. He has to meet someone from the University, has to see his publisher about corrections of his new play, makes a telephone call to Switzerland, complains about the two hundred pounds telephone bill, says Teresa is extravagant, that she spent too much money on her holiday in the South of France, now there isn't enough money for the pressing bill. His secretary vacuums the carpet; Teresa prepares a tasty cold lunch.

He is trendily dressed; she looks more like an anonymous housewife. She says she'll have to take half a Mandrax before starting the ironing; Adrian needs a clean shirt and he's very fussy about his shirts. The children, seven and fourteen are at school.

They consider themselves liberated sexually, he allows her maximum freedom, but she says she still tends to get jealous of him. They've been together for twenty years and are warm in their exchanges.

Drugs play an integral part in their relationships – they are both junkies.

****

"Heroin takes the sexual urge right away from me, and from most women. It also, incidentally, makes you stop menstruating. I didn't menstruate for a year, and if you forget about sex for years and years and then you start to get sexless, you don't care how you look, how you smell, you don't give a shit, all you do is . . . we may have made it twenty times in four years. But I conceived my eldest son while I had quite a habit going. And then I stopped at seven months, so he wouldn't be hooked. I just levelled off and I stopped and he was the most perfect child.

"Then of course you start again and then . . . it's mostly guilt that made me give it up, because I had Brent, and he was beginning to look at us askance, you know, when he was about six, because everything was going to hell – peeing into milk bottles because I couldn't walk down to the bathroom. The place stank, it was disgusting. I just had to kick, I felt so guilty, and Brent, he thought this was the way it was. He was just a little kid crouching in a corner of a dark flat, never going out to the park.

"Now we use it quite a lot again but we know how to handle it – it no longer uses us. And then of course when you have the money to buy it, that makes a lot of difference.

I've had a build-up of sexual incidents throughout my youth. You know, when I was thirteen I used to love horses. I lived for horses, like Elizabeth Taylor in *National Velvet* did.

"I used to fantasize about getting a job like a man to ride horses. I had a wonderful time with horses. I went into a stable once and a fellow was there, a spade, a stable man, and I was looking for this horse all by myself and he said, do you want to come in and he started feeling me and I felt . . . I was always afraid of embarrassing people, and I wouldn't actually admit that it was happening, and then I said, well I've got to go now, thanks a lot for the horse. I didn't say get your hands off me, you bastard, I just gave him a smile.

"And then my father had a friend who was a famous disc jockey, and I worshipped this man, and the guy took me to his bedroom once, said he had comic books and after a while he . . . pushed my face into his cock. My eyes were swimming with tears, I didn't know what to do, couldn't think of anything, and he . . . 'just give me a little kiss' . . . and it was horrifying. My eyes were brimming with tears, I mean, I was trying to read this comic book and I couldn't see it. I had worshiped him and had been so disillusioned . . . I mean people you worship didn't do things like that. He did it so grossly. I was so disillusioned and I called my mother, and she got worried and called my father. I expected him to say, get out of here, but he was embarrassed and they just said, well he's drunk. My father was just . . . I felt bitter towards him . . . just as disillusioned about him.

"I like my father although he was a real bastard, especially to my mother. He was all charm to the outside world and he'd come home and was completely different as soon as he closed the front door. He was nasty to my mother, he treated her like dirt, but to everyone he was the most charming man in the world. He also tried making love to me once – drunk – when I was seventeen.

"I was sitting on the floor watching television; mother was out somewhere. Father gets drunk and comes up behind me and we're both watching television and talking about it and he sort of puts his knees around my back and I felt him going hard and I just eased away and that's as far as it went. He was very embarrassed because he was always very uptight about sex.

"Adrian allows me a lot of freedom. He's a man who's made himself not jealous because he thinks it's an emotion we must discard. And he behaves like that, he's fantastic about that; he says, why don't you do it here, why don't we both. I'll go upstairs and you do it here. And I say, look you can fuck anybody you want, male or female, but just don't let me hear about it, I don't want it here.

"On one occasion I was pregnant too and feeling really ugly and he was up late. I woke up in the middle of the night and he wasn't there, and I heard strange noises upstairs and I went up. And there was this sexy chick who was here the night before, up here with him. So I went back to bed and in the morning I went up to him and said, will you tell your friend to FUCK OFF!!! You know, I was green, I was *livid*.

"I did that and I watched her get dressed and I watched her get out, you know.

"I don't always feel like fucking. I get involved in housework or something and I don't always feel like fucking. After twenty years it takes a little extra. With my husband, if he finds that someone else is interested in me, it perks him up a little.

"But I feel pretty free with him. I mean sometimes I pretend a little, I sometimes pretend that I'm satisfied when I'm not, or sometimes I get it over with because I'm tired. And because I'm also a middle-class little girl I do it just to make it nice for him if I'm not feeling sexy.

"Since I first heard you were doing this book I've been thinking about it, and I thought, my God, I don't have any fantasies, but of course I do. Bondage.

"I remember when I was about four or five, and this is one of my first memories – my mother went off one afternoon and left me with this woman next door and she went out for cigarettes and I immediately took off all my clothes, somehow tied my hands behind my back and got under a chair. So when she came back her face turned red. She was all a fluster and said, now dear, we mustn't do that, must we? And I'm not aware of having felt the slightest bit guilty, otherwise I wouldn't have allowed myself to be found.

"And then later, when I was seven, I used to get into bed – in my own little bed, by myself, with a chain, and I used to put this chain around my feet and wrists and I'd move it around and I still didn't know what I was doing. And then I started to fantasize. I used to imagine myself like . . . like you see in the comics – Lady Batman with big tits.

"Recently I went with a guy who I would never ever have been near. He's been after me and after me, and he happened to be living in our guest room at the time, and every time Adrian went out it was pant, pant, pant, you know.

"Suddenly one afternoon I'd had a Mandrax and I started getting sexy. The fact that he was so repulsive excited me. I said, all right, we'll do it. This is what you have to do: you've got to tie me in this chair. And my clothes – I made my clothes sort of look ripped open, like the pictures in the old fashioned magazines. And we did it and it was very, very exciting, although I would never have made it with this cat in a million years. The very idea of being repulsive, that's another purely sexual thing. I find that a fat man or a really repulsive man turns me on sexually – as long as I don't look close. But I don't want to know them afterwards.

"I don't get turned on by blue movies. I used to go out with this American when I was twenty; actually I used to work for him. A great big repulsive fathead and he was always after me like American bosses are. I usually hide but I hoped he was going to find me.

"One day he goes, hmmm, I've just got some films in, you want to see them? So I said alright and they were dirty films. One was a cartoon, a famous cartoon, but it was filthy: snakes climbing up cunts and arses; and the other had a plot.

"A woman goes into a – this turned me on so much – she goes into a ladies room and starts masturbating with a Coke bottle open end up; and so naturally it gets stuck and she tries to get it out and tries to get it out, and in the end she has to say, hey nurse, can you please ring a doctor, I'm in a terrible mess. Don't come in, but send a doctor. They take her to hospital . . . anyway it has a close-ups of the doctor at work and then of course three doctors, and they climb up on her, one after the other after they get the Coke bottle out, and she's writing, and that turned me on so much, and I really fucked the fat American. I was just out of my mind with sex, because he was so disgusting.

"I don't fantasize much when I'm fucking. I know people do. I masturbate a lot and I don't feel at all bad about it; I just do that any time I feel like it. If I'm reading a book and I'm feeling sexy and I come across a sex passage, then I read the passage while I'm masturbating, and whatever that fantasy is I go along with it. Or if my hand is there and I happen to feel sexy I do it, but then it's just groovy, I don't think of anything, I just do it. But I've also done it when I've had the house to myself, totally alone. I've dressed up, again bonds, tie the breasts tight, funny costumes out of scarves, and I stand in front of the mirror, spread my legs across the mirror and masturbate and watch myself and act it out – the whole fantasy of being tied, raped, forced, hurt, fucked."

VALERY

Valery is a twenty-seven year old American psychotherapist. Cerebral and conscientious, she handles other people's neurosis; and tries to handle her own with a level head.

Recently divorced from a Turk she is, at present, having a satisfactory affair with an Englishman.

Her speech is the verbal interpretation of her life style. She appears to analyze and to dissect every action (which in my opinion stifles instinct and causes a full-circle return to the original problem).

She comes from parochial circumstances – a Peyton Place type of environment, where the girl who loses her virginity before she gets married is disgraced. But Valery is the girl who got away, who was too intelligent for the town, too large for the parish: a pioneer who goes into the world in cashmere sweaters, a string of pearls and a neatly tied ponytail, with courage, integrity, good intentions and armed with an excellent university degree.

For the last three months she's been in charge of a halfway house, an institution which is a voluntary transition between society and a mental home. A mansion (run on funds from the Social State), which silently looms in an unkempt garden tucked away in a deserted leafy corner of ghostly suburbia, that houses twenty young inmates and their wardens.

The inmates are people who have nowhere to go, except back to the family which was a probable cause of their original break-down. Here they lived communally, with private bedrooms and a friendly young shrink and her helpers to see them through the numerous bad times.

Her large, cream-painted bedroom doubles as an office – a bed against one wall disguised as a settee, a mahogany cupboard, a wicker chair on a nondescript rug; a post card of a winter scene on the wall. Under the shuttered window sits a small round table with two chairs neatly flanking it.

I feel I'm sitting in a hotel room for people in transit. Outside the spring day passes unnoticed.

She's proud of the mansion, take me around. Everywhere is dark oak. The only sign of life is in the kitchen and in the individual bedrooms – most of which look as though a hurricane had just hit them.

She says: "Come and have a look at our living room, it doesn't get used much, I don't know why."

Like in an outmoded boarding house, settees with dead springs line the walls; the air is musty, projecting drab. I say, I know why it doesn't get used, it's dull, and she exclaims "One of the house rules is no decorating." Right, I thought, why put colour into drab lives?

She talked openly about herself, her universal father problem, her view that every woman had rape fantasies, when the telephone rang.

Valery told the caller that the boy, one of the patients, would have to go because he was having a negative effect on the house. He didn't want to work; he wanted to stay in bed in the morning, a habit which was very disturbing for anyone else.

It transpired that one of the house rules was that these patients, who had just come out of the hell of a lunatic asylum, have to get a regular job within three weeks of applying for residency.

She then went on to say that the main reason why he would have to leave is that he had broken the strictest rule: patients and anyone else living there were prohibited sex on the premises.

How different, I thought, this is from Laing's, Kingsley Hall[3] ,where the patient's freedom to do as they pleased was sacrosanct.

I was surprised at the change in her voice when she was on the phone; how stern she suddenly seemed to become, but when I thought about it, it made sense.

She herself had been qualified by the system, had spent many years going through the process and had become institutionalized. Although she's brighter than her colleagues, because she comes from a fresher, more progressive country, it's still the same. She's been churned out by factories where dreamers are termed negative and feminine, and where the best worker is of most use to his country. To the Stare. The robot that runs the smoothest and brings in the highest profit for the exploiter.

She came back to talk to me, relaxed and said she was against the rule, that things are much more liberal in America. She knows her policy of 'if you do it, don't let me know,' perpetuates the same game, the same sneakiness, the same shame, the same guilt. She said she would like to have the rule changed and was working towards the change – but her employers are not making discussions available. She sees the fault of the system but she knows she'll never beat it. She wants to continue her career; she likes what she's doing so she allows herself to be drawn in, blinkered against colour and poetry. But poetry is written by madmen, not by the curators who are available to them twenty-four hours a day.

When we finally got onto the subject of sex, she didn't come across as being up-front about her fantasy and I had to coax her a lot. She told me she had done a thesis on female sex fantasies and

---

[3] In 1965 Laing started a psychiatric community project at Kingsley Hall, where patients and therapists lived together.

that practically all the books she'd read on the subject had been hyped up male chauvinist products —
even the ones written by women. But then when given a chance to talk, to level, so that there might
be a book which dealt with the truth, true to her analytical nature she intellectualized about the
Oedipus complex and the collective unconscious.

****

"I've worked as a therapist in mental hospitals, never before in a residential centre. Here I'm living-in and I'm on duty twenty-four hours a day. I go to the bathroom or the kitchen for coffee and it's continuous. It's not the same way when you do therapy, when somebody comes in and you see them for an hour and they leave and where they go you don't know — it's their problem.

"I had a breakdown myself, when I was nineteen. I wasn't in a hospital because my breakdown came in a very socially accepted form. I was a compulsive eater and I slept about seventeen hours a day. You don't get sent to a hospital for that. I mean, I wasn't going to destroy myself or anybody else, my behaviour was social.

"You know a lot of people get sent to mental hospitals because of their social behaviour — people don't like the way they are acting. I was one of the lucky ones who didn't have to go, and that made a lot of difference in terms of my own self-image.

"I was extremely physical as a child and very into a heavy body thing that manifested itself in terms of being able to run fast and swim and wrestle. When I was fourteen I was on the tumbling team, I was on the swimming team. My fantasies at eleven, twelve, were of someone putting their arms around me, and then when I was sixteen I fantasized myself to an orgasm.

"I was with a foreigner, a tall, dark, handsome stranger who carried me away.

"I started masturbating and then I stopped because it excited me so much, and at the time I think that was the best way to handle a small-town situation, because a girl who did get in touch with her sexual feelings would get crucified.

"At eighteen I went to university and I thought all girls were virgins. Well, I found out that fifty percent of them were from California and none of them were virgins. I was really shocked. I mean all that swimming and all that eating and all that exercise and all that fight to be a nice girl and then I found out that none of the nice girls I knew were virgins!

"I've just got my divorce papers today, in Turkish. It's really interesting, this weird fantasy I've had, a recurring fantasy all my life from about the age of four, of running away or being kidnapped by a foreigner – and if I imagine myself in an Indian tribe it would be someone from a foreign tribe; if I was a cowgirl it was somebody from a foreign ranch; if I was an earthling it was somebody from Mars.

"I grew up in a small town. There weren't any foreigners; I don't know where I picked it up. It started at an extremely young age, and as I got older it became more sexual fantasy and I think when I got married I acted out the fantasy – it was a good way of hiding my incest fantasies.

"My husband was short and dark, my father was very tall and blonde and American, and yet they were remarkably similar, which I used to hide from myself for a long time because he looked so foreign.

"Jung says it's a reappearing archetype, even being acted out in particular cultures where the virgin girl was taken to the temple and a total stranger comes to make love with her and then leaves, and the purpose of the archetype, he says, is to work to get rid of the father fixation.

"I didn't get in touch with my incest fantasies until my father died. I'd been through a lot of therapy but I couldn't get in touch with a thing. Apparently they were just too frightening to get in touch with while he was still alive. After he died I started having all kinds of dreams of my elbowing my way between my mother and father; and then I started remembering, as a child, age fifteen, walking around nude around my father. Even all the therapy I'd been in, I hadn't remembered that until he died. And then I started putting things together and thinking, no wonder . . . I mean, my mother was incredibly hostile to me and I'd been the perfect daughter in every way, except I was fat. Which was a way of shitting on her.

"I was married ten months; it didn't work out at all. It was so totally impossible in Istanbul. You don't have all your cultural props which people depend on so much; you don't even have your language. To find any kind of meaningful work is totally impossible and the weather is so incredibly hot you can't even go outside, so it's very frustrating for people who want to use their energy. You really have to force yourself in a country like that.

"I don't have fantasies when I'm screwing. I can have masses and masses of orgasms. I like to screw with my eyes open, I like lights on. I don't need to fantasize; reality for me is quite good enough. But sure I've had fantasies about having a couple of men and just screwing for hours and hours and hours.

"The kind of men I fantasize about are not men who degrade women but men who just accept me, so it isn't a degrading situation. Probably like my sex researcher – I knew this lovely man who was a sex researcher. He was very liberated himself and was old enough and secure enough that he didn't have the typical male hang-ups, the male ego trip. He was in touch with a lot of his femininity and he could respond to my masculinity, which was a tremendous help.

"With him . . . the only time I've had . . . I don't know if you could call it a fantasy, in fact I don't think I would like that term on it.

"When sex had been fantastic with him – and this only happened a couple of times that it's been so incredible, and I've had orgasm after orgasm – it just goes on and on – where I really started getting into an archetypal feeling. The more I lose my head the more I get into an unconscious sexual thing where I feel he's like a universal man – of all ages. I feel he's an archetypal man, and it loses the personal thing. And he's got this hair on his chest and his back; and all the hair is coming across his back and I just felt the hair and I felt like it was a caveman and that we were going back thousands of years . . .

"I do think we have a collective unconscious, and the sex thing, when it gets like that, I don't think it's a fantasy. I think part of it is getting in touch with something collective in the sexual experience."

VERONICA

Veronica is thirty; divorced with two children. She owns a boutique in Chelsea. Her clothes, her attitude, her life-style are very 'now' – a natural advertisement for her business. She's very much into the revolution that is taking place in the minds of women.

****

"The strongest fantasies for chicks who, as it were, are not attached to one man, always seem to revolve round some kind of oral intercourse rather than straight sex. In effect if a guy doesn't have an imagination, then he's just not a good lay. He could be very good genitally perhaps, and keep the thing going, but it's still a straight fuck and that just ain't enough.

"I've talked in detail with various chicks that I know who are very upfront about their sex life, and there is a lot of rejection of lovers on the basis that they are not into any form of oral stimulation. I mean the revolution that's taking place in women's heads is that this can be and is like the grooviest way of fucking. Once having, as it were tasted the forbidden fruit, the idea of doing without it is just like, you know, if a man is that uptight or that strung-out, forget it. I mean if he finds it, you know, an embarrassment, that there is a sort of inhibition there, as I said, forget it. But actually it's an inhibition that exists in so many men . . . the men don't seem to have any imagination.

"One's fantasies seem to grow as one's experience broadens, encompassing everything. I remember one guy who was a Lieutenant Colonel in the army, years and years ago, turning me on to Vaseline, and I really had an incredible trip with Vaseline, like nothing I've ever known. I sometimes recreate that trip, because I've never ever come across a guy who's ever mentioned Vaseline since then, and I'm really quite shy so I wouldn't mention it either.

"There was a very beautiful pop singer that I lived with for a while who was bisexual, and he was really, really, really into sex as a sort of great theatrical drama. He didn't fuck very often, but when he did he really got it together.

"I once remember him stimulating me manually and I was lying back with my eyes closed, really digging it, and then I opened my eyes and at the same time as he was doing this to me with the one hand he was doing it to himself with the other. And I opened my eyes and as I did that there was this great fountain, and that was just such a flash and I was really cross with myself for not having got into it. And I recreate that trip in my head, but like I get into it all the way. I really create that, not just seeing the end of it.

"Oh, for instance, when one fantasizes, one might start out thinking in terms of the actual physical appearance of the guy. The picture that generally comes out is a sort of round about region of six-foot one, very slim-hipped but very sort of chunky-shouldered with certainly long hair and almost certainly a beard. And as a sort of dream-state level you can always, always visualize a really enormous prick, and that's really quite silly because a big prick isn't where it's at. It should be somewhere nicely in the middle.

"This actual creation of the person, this demigod, if you like, is in itself stimulating. And you then just move on to the location, and I guess the location is quite important. It certainly wouldn't be a bed; it's much more likely to be a floor in front of a fire, or in the woods, or a tent maybe, but more than likely rustic.

"I have the recall of one incredibly glorious scene of making it on the Scottish moors spending the whole day absolutely stark naked, not seeing a soul, fucking in the streams and fucking in the sheep pens and fucking on the heather up on the top of the hill. Just naked with the sun all day.

"And one would certainly imagine almost immediately a very high state of eroticism, where you're really very turned on – the sensation of one's body, the actual primary sexual characteristics, the erogenous centres such as ears and tits become secondary.

"One actually creates a sort of mental image of a very aware cunt, wet and turned on, and one brings in all the pleasurable sensation that one has experienced – the dream of complete and total orgasm, which is long and drawn out, and as intensive for as long a period as possible.

"Sexual acid experiences are just so dynamite. I get sort of a million orgasms streaming through my body, and I lie in front of the fire with my stereo headphones on, listening to Stray Cat Blues, and I just come and come and come. And I don't have to move – just lie there just completely relaxed and suddenly there's a sexual energy just pouring through my body and it's happening in a sort of visual sense that whatever is projected on my mental screen is also happening in my body. Only it's projected in an abstract way onto this mental screen and the music and it are completely and absolutely one; and it's perhaps in the form of energy vibration: light flows, streams – things like that.

"But at the same time it's completely without any effort at all, and I have one orgasm after another – it's just pumping its way through my body.

"But there's no sort of erotic imagery attached to it, none at all, and it is a total fantasy because it is a completely mind-created sensation, because your body is lying there just completely relaxed. "

VIRGINIA

Virginia is an only child from a run of the mill environment.

Tall and lanky, she's pale of complexion; her blonde hair tumbles to her shoulders. She's shy, passive, introverted, sensitive; somewhat dull. A fifteen-year-old teenager who rebels against family rule: smokes dope, takes pills, acid, gets pissed on red wine, and dances wildly at numerous parties.

Her mother, in her late forties, is a housewife. The father, ten years older than his wife, is an engineer. They live in a large block of flats in a four room apartment in Shepherd's Bush. They'd been there, she said, for as long as she can remember.

She goes to the local school, hates it; talks in the jargon which is fashionable amongst her friends. (And which at times I find hard to decipher.) Much of her social activity takes place in the nearby park. She would like to live in the country and be a tree doctor after she gets her 'O' levels, she said. And yes, she's had sex with two boys.

During the hour long interview she mostly gazed out of the window with bovine, sleepy eyes, volunteering minimal, un-detailed information, taking a long time to answer my questions in a low-keyed voice.

****

<u>PARENTS</u>

Hanja: "Does their marriage work?"

Virginia: "They seem to get along now. Like when I was very young, you know, like every night they used to have great big flaming rows; somebody would walk out of the house . . . not come back until the next morning. But now it never happens at all."

Hanja: "Did it upset you?"

Virginia: "Yeah, a hell of a lot. I thought whoever was going was going forever . . . I'd never see them again."

Hanja: "Do you communicate with them?"

Virginia: "I don't talk to them at all because my mother is so uptight about it, like there are some things I'd never dare tell my mother, but I think I might tell my father.

"I'd like to be very open with my children; like sort of be more of a friend than a mother, you know. I think that if I had a child I'd like it to be able to tell me everything."

Hanja: "Does your mother know that you've had sex?"

Virginia: "No!!!!"

Hanja: "What do they want you to do?"

Virginia: "They want me to wait till I'm sixteen, and then it's to be done with contraceptives."

Hanja: "Don't you use contraception?"

Virginia: "No."

Hanja: "Aren't you worried about becoming pregnant?"

Virginia: "Not really, I don't think about it."

Hanja: "What would you do if you became pregnant?"

Virginia: "Have a baby, I suppose."

Hanja: "How would you keep it?"

Virginia: "I expect I'd leave school . . . ask my parents to help, I suppose."

Hanja: "Do you like living at home?"

Virginia: "Not really, I don't like the restrictions . . . and having to do housework . . . not being allowed to go out until I've done the washing, instead of doing it in my own time."

SCHOOL

Hanja: "What do you think of school?"

Virginia: "School's a drag."

Hanja: "Why?"

Virginia: "Incredibly boring. Like they always do the same, they don't do anything interesting at all, you know."

Hanja: "Why don't you leave?"

Virginia: "I want to do my 'O' levels."

Hanja: "What about marriage?"

Virginia: "I don't think I want to get married really. If you get married and it's a failure, it's such a hassle to get out of it. I'd really dig to have children, though."

Hanja: "Do you like living in London?"

Virginia: "No. There's too many people you don't know. I think it would be nice living in the country because, you know, I like that sort of thing where everybody knows what everybody is doing. Everyone is so unsociable in London."

DRUGS

Hanja: "Do you take acid?"

Virginia: "Yeah."

Hanja: "A lot?"

Virginia: "Yeah."

Hanja: "Have you got something from it?"

Virginia: "Not yet, no. Like we just sort of loon off places. I'd like to really sit down and get something together, but I haven't you know."

Hanja: "Does it frighten you at all?"

Virginia: "No. I've got to the point where I couldn't really freak out 'cause I'm used to unusual and scary things happening. But I don't like to trip in big crowds."

Hanja: "Do a lot of kids use dope in your school?"

Virginia: "About one third are heads, one third straight and one third skin-heads."

Hanja: "Do skin heads smoked dope?"

Virginia: "They tend to go more for Mandies and speed."

Hanja: "How can you afford it?"

Virginia: "My grandmother is really rich and she lives in this great big house and she leaves money lying around and she's very absent minded. That's how I can afford it."

SEX

Hanja: "What do you think about sex?"

Virginia: "I don't have an opinion about sex actually."

Hanja: "When did you first make love?"

Virginia: "I can't remember . . . must be last year."

Hanja: "Was it good?'

Virginia: "Yeah . . . I enjoyed it . . . its good."

Hanja: "Did you have an orgasm?"

Virginia: "Yeah."

Hanja: "How come you've only done it twice?"

Virginia: "I just haven't fancied anyone else."

Hanja: "How old was he?"

Virginia: "Sixteen."

Hanja: "Had he done it before?"

Virginia: "No."

Hanja: "Did you tell your friends about it?"

Virginia: "Yeah. But we don't talk about it much. We know it's there and someday it's going to happen. But some guys like they don't care about you . . . they just want you for sex, which is a drag, you know."

Hanja: "Do you ever think of them just for sex?"

Virginia: "Yeah . . . I suppose I have."

Hanja: "Do you think there's a character difference between man and women?"

Virginia: "No . . . there isn't. I think the reason girls are sort of meant to play with dolls because that's just sort of been set down. Boys go off and play wars and all that. Yeah, it just evolved that way, you know. You just tell your children, here's a doll, play with it."

Hanja: "I don't know how you feel about talking about sex."

Virginia: "Oh, I don't mind at all."

Hanja: "When you go to bed with somebody, why do you do it?"

Virginia: "Uh . . . oh . . . well, I suppose to enjoy myself."

Hanja: "Is there any particular environment that you'd like to be in when making love?"

Virginia: "I'd prefer to be out . . . in the country."

Hanja: "Before you ever had sex did you ever imagine how it would be or what would happen and how you'd like it?"

Virginia: "Yes. It was completely different . . . I didn't think it was going to be sort of emotional, so excitable."

Hanja: "Do you think sex and love are interrelated?"

Virginia: "Yeah . . . but we weren't at all affectionate with each other afterwards."

Hanja: "Did you want to be?"

Virginia: "Yeah."

Hanja: "Why didn't you?"

Virginia: "I don't know . . . shy, I expect."

Hanja: "Do you have any ideas or dreams or fantasies of what you would like sexually?"

Virginia: "I used to have fantasies when I was younger. When I was eleven or so I used to have fantasies of being trapped down to a bed and things. Yeah . . . I can't remember too much about them. I must have been younger than eleven. Shit. Oh yeah, have you seen the film the Boston Strangler? Like that sort of thing. Raped and then strangled."

Hanja: "Do you like getting hurt?"

Virginia: "No."

Hanja: "Did you have those fantasies before you saw the film?"

Virginia: "Oh yeah. I had them when I was very young. I think they were in me before I came into contact with anything like . . . but my father's been getting *Playboy* for as long as I know. I don't know whether it just came from me or whether it came from that."

Hanja: "Do you think it matters when you're very young looking at magazines like *Playboy*?"

Virginia: "No, I don't think so really."

Hanja: "Do you read pornography?"

Virginia: "Yeah . . . I've read some books and magazines."

Hanja: "What do you think about it?"

Virginia: "I don't think there's anything wrong with them. Like some people would really dig to look at a book like that, others wouldn't. Lately I've had fantasies about chicks. And like, you know, when I was much younger like, you know there being two of us and sort of playing boyfriend and girlfriend sort of thing, and I think, yeah . . . it just builds up from there . . . fancying a chick. But the fantasies don't sort of go very far because I could never imagine myself doing it . . . you know. The thought just comes into my head, maybe if you have a really good friendship – like with a guy you sort of get romantic and things and that's okay – but if you want to extend your affection into sexuality with a woman everybody sort of says you're queer, makes you feel peculiar, you know, you sort of can't do it. I think that's why, you know."

YVONNE

Seventy-four year old Yvonne chars in a recording studio: she looks fifteen-years younger than her age and exudes energy as she dances to the music while she sweeps the floor. The full volume which pounds into my brain and hurts my ear-drums doesn't seem to bother her. She chats, jokes, and speaks loudly in a foreign accent. The sound engineers smoke dope; she refuses the joint, saying she's never been able to inhale, but accepts a glass of red wine from the producer; then goes to the pub next door, brings back toasted sandwiches for everyone, makes coffee in the studio kitchen, gives her opinion on the music. Her gray hair is pulled back in a bun; her round face speaks of good natured as do her bespectacled, lively black eyes. She laughs and laughs, showing horsy teeth; her short, stocky body is strong. Everybody in the studio loves her: she's part of the group.

I ask her shyly if she'll talk about her sexual fantasies. "Sure dear," she says enthusiastically. We make an appointment to meet at her flat.

Her bed-sitter is in an airless, dark, damp basement in a seedy building in a characterless street: a non-residential area almost exclusively utilized during the day by office workers.

A couch which doubles as her bed, two standard sofas, a green rug, and several small coffee tables covered with lace doilies and many framed photographs of her children, grandchildren, herself when she was much younger and her family in Belgium. Well cared for rubber plants, potted violets, and ferns all giving an impression of warm overcrowding. The sparkling-clean bathroom, she tells me, has only been installed a few years ago after much pressure on her part.

In the diminutive kitchen yeast pills, organic medicines, herbs, vitamin C, brown rice and potted herbs crowd on each other. After our talk she was going to the Health Food Fair which had opened the previous day.

She likes to go to the cinema, spends time in the pub, but finds that usually she can't communicate with her contemporaries. She admits to finding people of her age bitter, nasty, afraid, cantankerous and gossipy.

Born in a village on the periphery of Brussels she's been living in London ever since she married her Irish husband.

She serves me jasmine tea.

******

"I've been by myself for twenty years now. I don't hate men, I tolerate them. I like men's conversation and I like men's company, but I don't want to know further than that. I regard sex . . . I can feel it in myself that it's not dead, but I don't want it. I sometimes think it would be nice to meet someone, a companion, nice and loving, but as soon as I start saying, he's a nice chap, why don't you bring him home, my husband comes right back, right into my mind I get him, and I revolt against him . . . a kind of revulsion inside me. The first thing that comes into my mind is, they only want you for sex purposes, and I don't want a person for sex purpose only. Sex without love for me . . . yes . . . you enjoy it the same . . . but it's not satisfaction.

"A few months ago a bloke had the cheek to come and say to me – he's younger, about 20 years younger than me – he has the cheek to come and ring my bell and says: "Yvonne, whenever you feel you want sex I can oblige. It's my duty to make you come."

"I could have hit him, but he's bigger than me, so I shut the door in his face. And he was an intelligent person because he was a house master . . . but he has no sense. Sex is not duty; sex is because you want that person. How can the brain of a person work so it thinks that it's a duty?

"My husband wasn't what you might call a very good man. Oh, there's not another person on the face of the earth, no matter what nationality, like my husband. I have wasted my time in every kind of way. No satisfaction in sex, no satisfaction in love, no satisfaction in having a good husband and father.

"Well I loved my husband when we first married and he killed absolutely everything . . . I mean right down to the respect I had for him, and by killing that he killed the lot. I've had so much to put up with. I've got five children by him and he's never treated me like a person . . . anybody look at me he'd punch them in the nose – because that belongs to me. He'd make me feel like a piece of furniture. Well, your dream gets broken I suppose. He was like an animal, if you understand what I mean . . . he wants it, no matter if you was half dead he had to have it . . . he called that my duty.

"Sex to me should be loving, tender, warm, beautiful. With flowers and poetry. How can men satisfy themselves in sex and then leave you behind? How can they make a person happy, how can they call that love?

"Well, you don't realize it at the time that you are not satisfied. I had to put up with him for thirty years and then I couldn't bear it any longer and it was finished. Now if you come and tell me he's dead, alright, the neighbour is dead too.

"When I first came to England I heard a woman saying that there was nothing on the face of the earth more disgusting than childbirth. And I thought, well I don't know if she's going barmy or if she doesn't understand, or if I'm unusual. I was very sentimental as a young girl and very home loving and I didn't mind having children because I love children. I don't regard them as sex, if you know what I mean.

"You see when I come to England I couldn't speak English at all and it took me quite a long time. In those days you wasn't allowed to speak about sex. You wasn't even allowed to mention period time. My husband said my period was a dirty thing. In Belgium it was different. When a girl becomes a young woman – the first period she had – the family gave her a little present and they make a special occasion, the whole family, men, women, boys; and they know she's a young lady now and they give her presents because they are thankful she has become a woman.

"In Belgium you talk about sex. When I was young they talked about sex more there than here now. They have jokes as well. Here they talk about sex as if you've got to shove it under the carpet or something. What's there to be ashamed of? And another thing – my father was at the birth of all us children, and I'm seventy-four, so that's not new, is it? Here it's new. Now why? He's the father, why can't he see the child born? I think if the father was to be at the child's birth they'll be better fathers and becoming better fathers they'll be better husbands and better lovers. But not such a coward as the ones who don't want to be there.

"Also I used to strip at the waist in one house I lived that had no bath. I always do, to wash every day, and I didn't think anything wrong, then my husband's sister said I was dirty. But I just washed myself!!! You see because my mind didn't work that way, I said: "I just washed myself, how can I be dirty? "Fancy doing it in front of the children," she said. "Do what in front of the children? I never done anything wrong in front of the children." "You strip," she said. Oh my God! So you have to feed your baby, and you strip to the waist and that's called dirty also. Now this I can't think why.

"Is sex dirty? Still, to some people it is because they make it. Like my husband. As I said he acted like an animal and therefore sex was dirty in his mind, except when he needed it and then it was a kind of my duty. But not lovable . . . It's so very difficult when you come across people like that . . . well, to put it plainly, they turn you off.

"But I think the young people, they're all right. I realize it more and more by seeing the young people. They are free, free of mind. But the older people . . . now here's a thing that shocked me. You know the last *Romeo and Juliet* with those two very young people? Well the trailer was on television, and they showed Juliet in the room and she goes to bed and he goes to bed and they both show that they are half naked. I was in the pub and we was talking. I said, oh that's going to be a lovely film, I hope I'm going to be able to go and see it (which I wasn't able to because I don't like going to the pictures by myself and I never found anyone who wanted to go and see it. But I should have gone by myself.), and they said, you call that a nice film? Dirty little stripper in bed. How vulgar. Now what was wrong? The man who made that film had guts to take two young people and make it real, and they call it dirty. What's there to be ashamed of being in love and having sex?

"Well of course I'm alone most of the time. I do go back to Belgium sometimes to see my sister, yes, and last year I went to Spain to see one of my sons who lives there. Well I don't mind where I live – there's good things everywhere. But I would like to see more of my children. The thing is, my family, I don't know whether they're trying to be funny or what is wrong with them, they say I talk too much, but that's because I'm so much alone that when I get the chance to have somebody, I think I chatter, chatter. They want to know why I talk so much. They don't realize that they talk just as much as me.

"Now another thing is a woman, when she has a child, she loves her child. Why a man is jealous of his children I don't understand. They start to think that they don't get the attention, but they do, you see, if they look at it properly, they do. You love your husband just as much as you love your children – I did – and the things he is able to do for himself, surely he don't expect you to do it when you've got youngsters that need to be attended to. That's where the man goes wrong; they don't want to do for themselves that which they are capable of doing.

"It starts with the mothers, doesn't it? I brought up four boys and one girl and I used to say: all right, you get up and you do that, you do this, and you do that. And one day Paul came in and said: "Not my job to wash up; Mary's job to wash up." "Mary's job to wash up?" I said. "Yes, it's Mary's job to wash up. She's a girl." So I said "What difference it makes, you're a boy and you eat like her, don't you? Every job has to be done by everybody, and you'll find out when you grow up."

"Now they've all turned out to be good husbands except Mike – he's like his father, he's got that bit of Irish in him that he expects a woman to be at home except when he wants her out. She waits on him, he stays in bed, she takes him breakfast. Because he's the lord of the manor he has his breakfast in bed. I say to that boy: who brought you up, for Christ's sake, that you turn out to be like that? I get so mad with him. It's her fault because she serves him and I've already told her. I said, "For a plate or rice a day you make a doormat of yourself."

"I heard a young black bloke in a pub once, what was he 28, 29? And his belief is that a woman's place is at home with the kids by the sink. I said, "If you was a son of mine," I said, "I'd clobber you. What makes you think a woman's place is at the sink? A husband's place is by his wife's when he's finished work and they go out together, and they do things together, but you people don't, and it takes the beauty out of love and sex."

"Now some women say if their husbands really loved them they couldn't go somewhere else . . . with another woman. In my feelings as a woman I think a woman can't do it. A woman feels guilty when she goes with somebody else because she's doing it without love, but a man, although he's in love with his wife, he can still go with another person because a man in his own mind wants a certain kind of satisfaction. A woman thinks there should be love on both sides, and that's why there are more women who are true lovers than men.

"Now if I think how I would like to make sex, it would be with a gentle man who really loves me and thinks of my pleasure as well as his. He would kiss me all over, like my husband never did, and tell me he loves me. And we would have this lovely sunny bedroom with lots of mirrors and flowers and wall-to-wall beige carpets. And there would be pink satin sheets on the bed."

CONVERSATION WITH R.D. LAING (London, May 1981)

We both slouch on the comfortable couch in his spacious study so elegantly created by his wife, Jutta, in barley tones and Asian rugs.

Ronnie's hung-over Charles Boyer eyes stare out through the bay windows, across the flower-patched front lawn, onto the birch whose ripe-plum tinted leaves curtain off most of the view of Eton Road. He heaves a heavy sigh that evokes a sense of loneliness in me. Or is it 'alones'?

There are books and papers everywhere: dropped here and there, despite of Jutta's brave efforts to keep everything in place. On the mantle above the fireplace sits a delicately carved, small bronze Buddha among other objects and photographs that please the eye, touch, and imagination.

Music sheets and albums are piled on top of the black Steinway whose ivory keys play such an integral part of Ronnie's being. Playing the piano is Ronnie's medicine. He is forever drawn to it.

The solid pine table in front of the window is cluttered with diaries, satin covered Chinese note-books, newspaper cuttings, elegant writing tools, a Victorian ink-well, a large copper ashtray, an empty glass left over from last night's party. Last night we sang. That was easy, but now we're going to talk and I'm feeling nervous.

Ronnie sighs and I wonder why I've let myself in for this . . .

HK: What is sexual fantasy?

RDL: Sexual fantasy is the free play of the imagination. There are sexual fantasies which seem to be generated in the act of sexual intercourse, in the course of it itself, and those fantasies that have to do with desire — imagining oneself into a situation in the first place that one isn't in actually. There's these things that one imagines that one might do that don't rise out of the actual experience of physical sex and intimacy itself. In some of these fantasies in your book people describe the way their minds actually go when they are making love, and then there are other fantasies which are part of someone's repertoire that they call on at any time, day or night. They don't necessarily motivate someone to do anything about them, they belong to a world of story books, fairy tales and such . . .

HK: Do any of them turn you on?

RDL: Well I don't know . . . maybe . . . I suppose . . . no, they don't turn me on.

HK: Can anything go in sexual fantasy?

RDL: If there is no objection to free play of the imagination then it's a straightforward free for all – every combination that there is can arise.

(Before we began the conversation Ronnie told me he would not speak about his sexual fantasies, but I go for it anyway)

HK: Do you have sexual fantasies?

RDL: Well I have a certain moderate sexual fantasy life. It's never been a very baroque one: that sort of persistent elaboration that say OOH – do you know the book?

HK: OOH?

RDL: OOH!

(At times Ronnie's Glaswegian accent foils me. But then I get it.)

HK: Oh, *The Story of O*?

RDL: Yes, *The Story of OOH*. Well that sort of mind that gets hold of something like that and then peruses it and becomes completely imbued by it . . . Well I've never been carried away that I can be affected . . . I've sometimes wondered whether the unfolding of a fantasy like that is the ordinary function of the unimpaired or uninhibited mind or whether that's a gift some people have more than others. It so often seems to be crushed into a situation that is spicy because it's *risqué*: it's dangerous or it is forbidden. I don't like to have to feed off artificially, socially conditioned danger or prohibition in order to get sexually turned on – somehow parasitically living off a pleasure that a lot of people condemn. Something that takes me off my course, as it where. . .

(Ronnie tops up our mugs with strong, percolated coffee and waits for me to say something.)

HK: Do you masturbate, or is this one of the questions I'm not supposed to ask?

RDL: Oh you can ask whatever you like! I'm going to make a point of not talking about my sexual fantasies because I'm going to keep that for writing about it myself – I don't see anything against this. If anyone is interested in reading that, I have my own account. Sexual fantasies are a commodity, so I'm going to, I hope, make some money out of them. So I'm going to hold them in reserve . . .

HK: You are going to make us curious . . .

RDL: Yeah . . .

HK: Do you use sexual fantasies in your therapies?

RDL: Well I don't know whether to say I use them, but they crop up as relevant quite often. Sometimes someone doesn't think they are relevant and I feel that they are and encourage them to explore them. There's a certain person who is quite immersed in sexual fantasies, and though they look at them from the outside they don't quite know what they are because they are always inside them. But it doesn't arise in therapy unless someone's sexual life is not working to their satisfaction. There's quite a few people who seem to be very unhappy, but their sexual life isn't always in a mess. You know I'm not a Freudian in the sense that I don't think that the sexual experience is always the nuclear area that's generating unhappiness. I'm not interested in what people's sexual fantasies are very much. All I need to do is face them with . . . what's usually messing them up is that they feel guilty about what they're imagining. I don't feel that I'm entitled to act as a sort of spiritual adviser and lay down the law that all is permissible. I think someone has to make *up* their own mind about that. But they've got to make their own mind up, because a lot of people are very miserable because they can't allow themselves to.

        (Having given up coffee we now drink wine.)

RDL: The commonest thing I would say with women – and with some men – that makes them unhappy about their sexual fantasies is that they feel guilty about imagining themselves being turned on erotically by alternative situations to the one they're in. Which is what imagination after all is very largely all about. It's imagining something else. And that means a feeling of guilt very often about being unfaithful to their current sexual partner who they ought to be thinking about, imagining, addressing themselves to. They're betraying the act of love!

        (His statement makes Ronnie chuckle out loud.)

HK: I've read recently that the Pope declare that committing adultery in the heart, in the desire and the imagination adultery.

RDL: That's a very big pull over many people. If a man ceases to fancy his wife, say, and wants to imagine himself fucking his neighbour's wife while he's fucking his own wife – he can't allow himself to do that. It's almost worse than fucking his neighbour's wife. He's been told that's a mortal sin.

HK: But then the mortal sin fascinates and excites him erotically.

RDL: Yeah, I suppose a lot of people are fascinated by what is forbidden.

HK: What are your views on 'mind adultery'?

RDL: What I think about it is very conditioned by the sort of understanding that someone has with their own sexual partner. Sexual fantasies and sexual practices are very much governed by basically known social issues – which is implicit or explicit agreement, understanding, undertaking, promises, vows, so called trust and then all the things that go under the term of faithfulness, of unfaithfulness ,or jealousy, or infidelity. When someone has made a contract with someone, whether it's a business contract or a sexual contract or whatever I may be, then the issue is whether you keep your side of it or not. Well that issue so overshadows the sexual that it's almost impossible to disentangle it. I've seen many people over the last 30 years, and just as much now as 30 years ago, both men and women agonize over this sort of thing. They can't see their way to . . . it makes them feel guilty, it destroys their own eroticism. That's one of the fantasy jams that are behind male impotence and so-called frigidity in women. There's one woman I've been seeing currently – she knocked her clitoris when she was 12 years old and the slightest touch on it, whether by her own hand or anyone else's is extremely painful. She says it really is painful – not only the clitoris is painful but there's feelings that seem to radiate from it that send pain through her. She's seen gynaecologists who can't see anything wrong with her, but it could be a sort of fibrous irritation. I suppose the nerve endings might be bruised – there's no way of telling . . .

HK: So she doesn't have sex?

RDL: Yes she does and it hurts her. And then she would develop a fantasy of fucking someone else – practically anyone else than the guy she's with . . . *aaahhh* (Ronnie's sighs seem to get heavier as the conversation proceeds), and then she feels that's a betrayal of their relationship and so that's a downer for her. Yet the pleasure only seems to come with a link of her imagining herself with someone else. That fills her with waves of pleasure. If she comes back to the present moment the impact is pain: and if she gets to the pleasure then she feels desperately depressed afterwards. Well that's the sort of situation people come to see me about. But I don't think God is particularly bothered with what someone's got in their mind when they are having either sexual intercourse or sexual fantasies. I just can't take it all that seriously, as a sort of desperate issue of mortal sin. That you're placing your soul in jeopardy. Oh goodness! I can't get with it.

I was brought up with that sort of thing without ever anything being said — the whole thing being taken for granted. This is the Protestant version of that. And how these things are being transmitted without words being spoken — and they certainly are — is, I think, an issue for people like me. Since masturbation is so bad in itself and fantasy in relationship to masturbation is making a total depraved pig of yourself — morally and spiritually, hmhmhmhmhmhm (big chuckle here).

I suppose my reason for not talking about my own sexual fantasies, at the moment is for two reasons. One is commodity, and the other — I don't know whether you regard this as justifiable — is a sense of self-protection. Since in some circles I'm a well known person I don't know whether I want to add to my already ambiguous public image my sexual fantasy. I don't like the way people deal with other people's sexual fantasies. You know, it goes without saying that any sexual fantasy that I might have at al would be immediately open to, by some people, condemnation and so forth. I don't know whether I want people to have that handle on me. But I don't know whether you think that's justifiable.

HK: Well I'm hardly here in the habit of a judge, Ronnie, but I do wonder why women like Judith Malina, Molly Parkin, or me, for that matter, are prepared to tell it all. I don't know if it's a form of exhibitionism or being extremely brave — it's certainly brave to put oneself on the line like that. I think it's something women do more than men — maybe that has something to do with brazen confrontation

RDL: Well you must feel that you want to, that it's important. You've got a sort of sense of mission about it – helping all the women to . . .

HK: . . . And men.

RDL: . . . And men to clear up their hang-ups. I'm' motivated that way myself.

HK: Of course it doesn't mean to say you're going to help anyone by telling them your sexual fantasies.

RDL: Yeah, I don't know whether it would make my own life easier or more difficult by making my sexual fantasies a topic or not.

HK: Okay, so we'll keep it a secret.

RDL: Don't you feel any sense of loss at giving away secrets of your own? Don't you like to keep something secret just to yourself and don't tell maybe anyone and get pleasure of the sweetness of the secret?

HK: No. I think that's a romantic sort of concept . . .

RDL: Romantic?

HK: I think these kinds of 'secrets' stop you from finding the real secret. I don't think that's the secret.

RDL: Well a secret is something which you keep secret, it's not the content of it.

HK: Sacred secret.

RDL: Secretum, secretion. Internal secretion means separating materials from the blood. Some people find secrets very burdensome: they don't like to have them.

(Ronnie rolls a joint and hands it to me)

RDL: There are all sorts of secrets: there are bitter secrets and tormented secrets, and secrets that people don't want.

HK: Yes, someone lays a secret on you and suddenly you're stuck with it. And if you tell your labelled as untrustworthy. But you didn't want to get landed with the secrecy in the first place. The rules have been made for you by the other.

RDL: Well as I said, there are all sorts of secrets. There's a secret that lovers have between themselves which can be extremely romantic – the secret romance, the secret love affair . . .

HK: Secrets one cannot betray . . .

RDL: I think how much secrecy goes on in sexual practice definitely affects one's view of what's going on in the psycho/sexual/social networks that one lives in. One way of construing all that sort of reality depends on how much weight you give to subterfuge and camouflage, secrecy and lies. Which is the impossibility I have of not ever knowing what to make of those statistics – what answers people give in those questionnaires. What resemblance that has with what's actually going on. Of course the depth of secrecy is elaborated on , and as you say, the sexual policy, as it were . . . that man, for instance, who was turned off by his wife and couldn't get turned on to her except by imagining himself having a sexual relationship with someone else. Couldn't tell his wife that, because he felt she'd be absolutely, completely outraged and furiously jealous if she thought he was fucking someone else in his mind when he was fucking her. He could either take a risk and say: look here, let's agree that when we make love our minds can be free, you go where you like, I'll go where I like. Our camaraderie in the sexual act is based on something deeper: it's based on a camaraderie of reciprocal freedom – that we are able to travel in our minds. If he could work something like that out with his sexual partner it would be different. But I don't get the impression that many couples manage to have achieved that candour between themselves.

(Ronnie sighs, then giggles. We both laugh.)

RDL: I think that in our society one cannot expect to have a run of perfect harmony of one's desires and availability and so forth. That's bound to happen it patches . . .

HK: If you're lucky!

RDL: If you're lucky. It's a terrible hassle if what one wants at the time is not easy to come by. It's a continuous process of adjusting one's desires to getting what's convenient. If one could imagine oneself never engaging in any sexuality and never missing it, wanting it, not having to have it, I've quite often wondered whether I'd trade that in for any sort of sexual life.

HK: I suppose we look for love through making love.

RDL: Ahhhh . . . I suppose so. There's something about the act of making love that makes a difference. Consummation. I can't think I could imagine, as it where, a passionate celibate relationship that some people go for as in the annals of chivalric romantic love. You know, you have an intense celibate relationship with your lady whom you call a loved one, but you practically never have a sexual relationship with her. You know the type of sexuality Stendhal describes in *De l'amour*, or Dante and Beatrice – *Vita Nuova* and *Divina Comedia*. Or there's those gorgeous ladies , maybe a courtesan or maybe a society lady at the opera, dressed up and in the boxes. Proust – all those sights and enchantments at a distance. Sight and sound is one thing, but the domain of love is touch, taste and smell. The visual sense tends to evaporate with me in the actual act of sexual intercourse. I like to sink into the situation through the actual sensations that are going on – the actual sensation of smell, skin, warmth, touch, textures, taste. I like to abandon the sight and sound. This has been influenced actually by the type of Buddhist meditation I have particularly cultivated. Seems a very dry one to some people, but it's very effective. Actually paying bare attention to the sensation that's happening. And through doing that, sort of going into it and to the other side of it – into where it takes one through it. Well, there's no doubt about it that that is certainly a gateway into a blissful state. And if one combines that state of bliss with the coloration of erotic pleasure – it's extremely pleasant.

www.ingramcontent.com/pod-product-compliance
Lightning Source LLC
Chambersburg PA
CBHW070033300526
45794CB00001B/470